M & E HANDBOOKS

M & E HANDBOOKS are recommended reading for examination syllabuses all over the world. Because each Handbook covers its subject clearly and concisely books in the series form a vital part of many college, university, school and home study courses.

Handbooks contain detailed information stripped of unnecessary padding, making each title a comprehensive self-tuition course. They are amplified with numerous self-testing questions in the form of Progress Tests at the end of each chapter, each text-referenced for easy checking. Every Handbook closes with an appendix which advises on examination technique. For all these reasons, Handbooks are ideal for pre-examination revision.

The handy pocket-book size and competitive price make Handbooks the perfect choice for anyone who wants to grasp the essentials of a subject quickly and easily.

THE M & E HANDBOOK SERIES

Business Systems

R. G. Anderson
FCMA, MInst.AM (Dip), FWSOM

MACDONALD AND EVANS

Macdonald and Evans Ltd.
Estover, Plymouth PL6 7PZ

First published 1977

© Macdonald and Evans Ltd. 1977

7121 0254 X

Printed in Great Britain by
Hazell Watson & Viney Ltd,
Aylesbury, Bucks

Preface

Business today is conducted in an age of economic crises and highly complex technology, imposing on business management the need to implement sophisticated business systems which accord with present day needs. The idea for writing this book originated during the course of conducting research on the changing scene of business systems, in preparation for a course of lectures: it was found that many developments were taking place and, accordingly, there appeared a need for a book to explain the current situation.

It is hoped, therefore, that this book will give students of business subjects an insight into present developments. From the author's experience of teaching on accountancy foundation courses, it is apparent that many students, particularly those from overseas, do not possess initial business experience. This creates a difficulty in understanding such subjects as Data Processing, which require a grasp of business systems in the first instance. One of the aims of this book is to remove this difficulty by, first of all, defining the nature of business systems, their purpose and objectives: the nature of non-financial and financial systems is then considered, before embarking on an appraisal of the conceptual aspects of business systems, database concepts, and the role of the computer in the effective operation of business systems.

The analysis of systems is then discussed in the development of clerical and computerised systems, indicating the approach of Organisation and Methods investigators and Systems analysts. The role of internal auditing and its association with business systems is also dealt with.

The book is eminently suitable for students studying for the Diploma in Administrative Management in respect of the papers relating to The Systems Approach to Administrative Management.

In addition, it should provide a valuable source of information for administrative managers, accountants and O. & M. investigators and systems analysts, for obtaining a wide appreciation of business systems which is so essential for the development and implementation of more effective systems.

In general, the book would benefit students preparing for the examinations of the following bodies:

The Institute of Cost and Management Accountants (I.C.M.A.).

The Institute of Administrative Management (I.A.M.).

The Institute of Practitioners in Work Study, Organisation and Methods (I.W.S.O.M.).

The Association of Certified Accountants (A.C.A.).

The Society of Company and Commercial Accountants (S.C.A.).

The Higher National Diploma in Business Studies (H.N.D.B.S.).

C.N.A.A. Degrees (relating to business systems).

This HANDBOOK is complementary to the author's Organisation and Methods, Data Processing and Management Information Systems and Corporate Planning and Control in the same series.

For the purpose of assisting students, a selection of questions are included in Progress Tests from The Institute of Administrative Management's papers, in respect of The Systems Approach to Administrative Management.

A number of case studies have also been included among the Appendixes, to demonstrate the practical aspects of points made in the text, or to illustrate important concepts in the development of systems for various types of business organisation.

In addition, Appendix II illustrates various flow-chart symbols which are used for the construction of procedure charts, procedure analysis charts, computer run charts and program flow charts. The reader is recommended to refer to the symbols when studying the various charts in the book.

September 1977   R.G.A.

Acknowledgments

I gratefully acknowledge permission to use past examination questions of The Institute of Administrative Management in respect of The Systems Approach to Administrative Management. I would also like to thank the following organisations for their co-operation and assistance:

Accountancy Age, Haymarket Publishing Ltd.: provision of information for the preparation of Case Study 2—On-line Building Society Operations, and Case Study 3—Catalogue Shopping in Retail Sales Operations.

W. & T. Avery Ltd.: permission to reproduce Fig. 43, Stages of Introducing a Computer system.

J. A. Crabtree and Co. Ltd.: permission to reproduce Fig. 33, Batch Processing Computer Configuration.

International Computers Ltd.: provision of information on computer package programs.

Patent Shaft Steelworks Ltd.: provision of information for the preparation of Case Study 1—Real Time Control of Steel Making and the provision of details of their on-line order-entry system.

Raytheon Cossor Data Systems: permission to reproduce Fig. 34, Airline Reservations and Ticketing System; Fig. 35, Tour Operators On-line Computer System; and Fig. 36, Stock Exchange On-line Computer System, together with relevant information on such systems.

Northern Software Consultants Ltd.: provision of information in respect of their Nominal Ledger package.

R.G.A.

Contents

List of Illustrations

List of Tables

CHAPTER I

The Nature of Business Systems and the Business Environment

THE NATURE OF BUSINESS SYSTEMS

1. Business systems and technology. Business today is conducted in both a highly complex technological, and economically critical age. The current economic climate poses a threat not only to the profitability of many businesses, but to their very survival. In an attempt to ward off this threat, many businesses have recognised the need to harness technology, not only to manufacturing processes but also to business systems, in a bid for higher productivity. By this means, it is hoped to stem the inflationary spiral since higher productivity generates lower costs of production and administration—which, if passed on to the consumer, results in stable prices for goods and services. Increases in productivity ward off price increases but, of course, productivity improvements do not just happen: they have to be striven for, normally by improving methods of production throughout the business, probably requiring investment in superior machines, both in the manufacturing and administrative functions.

Enlightened business managers have had the vision to see the need for business operations to be conducted within the framework of sophisticated "space-age" systems which, in general, may be defined as *administrative* systems. Incorporated within such systems are advanced "weapons-support-systems" (to use the phraseology of the armed services) which, in the medium to large-sized business, often takes the form of a computer complex of varying degrees of sophistication. This, to a greater or lesser extent, enables the administrative functions of a business to be automated.

A computer complex does not exactly adopt the status of a command centre, but it certainly does trigger-off commands from management, as it is a valuable aid to management decision making. This is so because, when a computer is dedicated to serving the needs of the whole business, or important operating areas, then the right type of information is provided exactly when and where it is required.

In many instances however, a computer complex does function as a communications centre, especially in the more advanced computing systems, as they incorporate networks of communication—lines connecting strategically-sited terminals to the computer (*see* Appendix III). By this means, a business with geographically-dispersed operating units can have access to information stored in a databank and, in some instances, major operating areas of a business can be controlled by on-line or real-time systems, whether steel-making, airline operations, stock-broking or banking (*see* IX).

Executives and other authorised personnel can also use time-sharing facilities for problem solving and corporate planning, as well as other on-line operations such as stock control and factory data-collection systems. In such instances, the type of operation is referred to as "conversational" or "interactive", because the computer responds to the requests or commands generated by the terminal user. The computer receives data signals in the form of "bits" (binary digits) and processes them, under the control of complex operating systems (software—mainly for the purpose of automating multiprogramming and concurrent batch and on-line processing operations) and application programs, at the speed of light (electronic speed), which allows a business to contend with the incessant demand for information by executives and other personnel. This enables them to control their area of responsibility more effectively because, by gaining access to key facts when needed, management are able to make well-balanced decisions.

The foregoing briefly describes how computers are widely used at the present time, or are in the course of development. The current scene is far removed from the age of the abacus and the quill pen and also from even more recent hardware, notably the forerunner to the computer—the punched-card installation. This is not meant to imply that all businesses should have a computer, or real-time system, but it *is* meant to imply that they should be armed with business systems and equipment suitable for their needs, so that they may operate as effectively as possible to ward off economic threats, so far as efficiency allows.

2. Galaxy of business systems. Business systems support the whole spectrum of business operations, including planning and launching a new product; planning production; paying wages; invoicing goods to customers; controlling stocks; scheduling aircraft; controlling costs, income and expenditure and purchasing materials.

There exists a whole galaxy of business systems, each of which is custom-built to suit the needs of individual businesses, which differ greatly, even between organisations in the same industry. In general, systems may be broadly classified as administrative, since they administer the various activities of the business which, in respect of a manufacturing business, covers production and marketing operations. Some types of business are mainly administrative, as they do not possess manufacturing operations and this applies to insurance companies, finance houses, building societies, travel agents and banks, etc. As most business organisations are structured on a functional basis, for ease of administration, applying the principle of specialisation, then many administrative systems are of a functional nature.

Business systems fall into two main categories, financial and non-financial, and Fig. 1 outlines the types of system which may

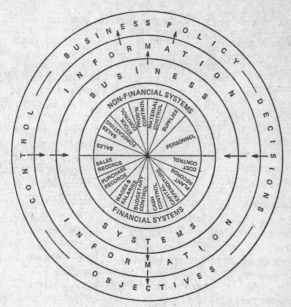

FIG. 1 *Galaxy of business systems.*

be found in these categories in a typical manufacturing business. Most systems tend to provide information as a by-product and together they form the information system of the business. Information systems are in reality a concept rather than separately organised systems, as systems in general generate information by the integration of additional procedures to the basic procedures for the provision of management reports.

It has already been stated that most systems are functional, serving the needs of specific functions, as single entities, but others may be designed within the concept of a "total" systems structure, embracing several functional systems, because in reality all business systems are related to each other, to a greater or lesser extent. This topic will be dealt with in greater length in VI.

Various systems have different characteristics, depending upon their nature; some may be classified as deterministic, probabilistic, open-loop or closed-loop, etc. (see Table I). Whatever the nature of a system, it is imperative that it should be dynamic or adaptive, so that it can respond to change in a flexible manner.

TABLE I. NATURE OF BUSINESS SYSTEMS

Type of system	Features	Characteristics
Organic	Dynamic self-organising systems which respond to change.	Computerised systems which allow parameters to be modified, such as in stock control systems, or which accept random transactions at random time intervals, as in real-time systems.
Mechanistic	Rigid and inflexible systems which do not respond to change.	Operate within a framework of procedural directives.
Deterministic	Systems whose results are predictable without error.	Not normally applicable to business systems which are of a probabilistic nature.

TABLE I.—*cont.*

Type of system	Features	Characteristics
Probabilistic	Stochastic systems whose results are predictable only within defined limits.	Normally applicable to business and economic systems whereby situations vary through chance causes.
Cybernetic	Systems with in-built feedback and control.	Includes systems which incorporate exception reporting and systems which maintain a state of "homeostasis", that is, a steady state despite "buffeting".
Closed-loop	Systems which communicate output for comparison with control parameters for the generation of error signals (variances from planned results).	Feature of cybernetic systems which have in-built control and feedback.
Open-loop	Systems which do not communicate output for comparison with control parameters.	Systems which do not incorporate in-built control and feedback.
Predictive	Systems which attempt to predict the future state of affairs.	Forecasting, budgeting and planning systems.
Planning	Systems which plan the use of and allocate resources to tasks.	Systems which establish guide lines and objectives for future action.

TABLE I.—*cont.*

Type of system	Features	Characteristics
Functional	Separately structured systems for the specific activities of various functions.	Systems which correspond with the functional organisation of a business.
Integrated	Combination of related functional systems.	Systems which transcend functional boundaries.
Total	Systems which embrace the whole or a major part of business activities.	Data input once only which updates all relevant files or data elements in a data base which may be accessed by all relevant functions.
Information	Systems which supply management with information for control and decision making purposes.	Systems which collect, process, compare and supply important facts of business operations in an appropriate time scale at the requisite level of accuracy.

This is essential in the modern world, as sociological, technological, economic and legislative factors are undergoing continuous change. It is essential, therefore, that systems be tuned to signals being transmitted in the current business environment (*see* Fig. 2).

3. Tuning business systems. To deal with changing circumstances, systems investigators are required and, in the larger business, O. & M. staff and systems analysts are employed for this purpose. They are mainly employed to serve the needs of administrative management, who are mainly too pre-occupied with daily operations to have time at their disposal for system improvements.

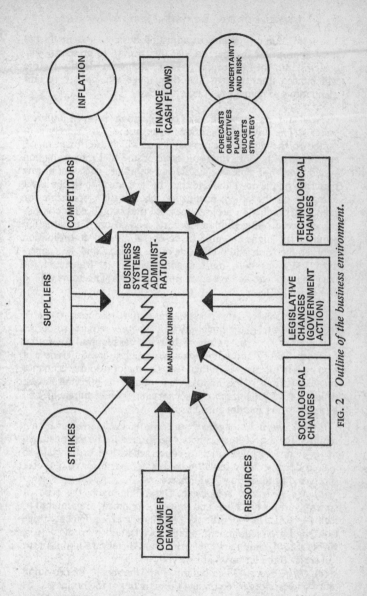

FIG. 2 Outline of the business environment.

The term "tuning" relates to adjusting business systems in the most appropriate manner, so that they accord to present needs. Systems staff investigate the present systems to identify factors which need improvement and they make appropriate recommendations to management (*see* X, XI).

4. Need for co-operation and co-ordination between different systems. The physical operations of a business are closely connected to the various business systems, which are, for instance, concerned with controlling stocks, to ensure that the production system does not suffer delays due to shortages of essential raw materials on the one hand and that the investment in stocks is not excessive on the other; production planning is responsible for preparing production programmes and the cost office for compiling and controlling production costs, and so on. This situation requires the highest degree of co-operation and co-ordination between the "nuts and bolts" side of the business and the "paperwork" side, as both must operate within the framework of business policy to achieve corporate objectives. This topic will be continued in II.

5. System resources. Business systems require resources to enable them to operate, in the same way that a factory requires resources and, what is more, the nature of the resources required are similar for both factory and administrative systems. The difference, of course, is in the manner of their use. The major resource is finance because without it, it is impossible to obtain the other resources: which are, personnel, office space, machines and equipment, and business forms and documents.

(*a*) *Personnel*. Managerial, supervisory and clerical staff are required for the various activities performed in the various business systems. Basic activities are concerned with recording data on source documents; calculating wages; preparing invoices, cost sheets and production schedules, etc.

(*b*) *Machines and equipment*. Depending upon the type of system, various machines and units of equipment are required to facilitate efficient operations. Machines and equipment range from mail-room equipment, filing cabinets, desk-top calculators, visible record computers, typewriters and dictating equipment, to full-scale computer installations.

(*c*) *Office space*. Office buildings are the means of providing office space, in order to conduct the activities of the business. The extent of this requirement is self-evident when one views the multi-storey office blocks which abound. Such space is required, not only for the provision of working space for personnel, but also for machines and equipment. Space is also required for conference facilities and document storage.

(d) *Documents and forms.* These are an essential element of business systems, as they are used as vehicles for recording and communicating information internally and externally. They are required for recording routine business transactions in respect of insurance premiums, hire-purchase payments, banking transactions, remittances to customers, goods received from suppliers, stores issues, wages, despatches to customers, inspection data, and order progress, etc. Forms, in general, embrace all "pieces of paper" including schedules and reports for purposes of management control and decision making. The wider category, therefore, includes payrolls, stock schedules, lists of account balances, product profitability reports, expenditure lists, budget statements, cash flow statements and balance sheets, etc. The manner in which they are produced ranges from the handwritten to the computer printouts (*see* II, 5).

THE BUSINESS ENVIRONMENT

6. Environmental perspective. The purpose of this chapter is to identify to the reader the broad spectrum of business systems rather than a detailed exposition, as this will be dealt with in later chapters. Therefore, to enable business systems to be viewed objectively in panoramic perspective, rather than restricted close-up, it is proposed to outline the environment in which businesses operate.

In the narrow confines of a particular business, it is important to appreciate that it operates by means of well-defined, efficient procedures, systems and methods. When a business consists of a number of associated companies, or dispersed operating units, then it is advantageous if such procedures, systems and methods are standardised as far as possible, thus facilitating efficiency, inter-firm comparisons and group consolidations.

7. Economic environment. No business exists in a vacuum and so cannot entirely control its own destiny, as it is subjected to external influences over which it has no direct control—it is in the "lap of the gods", as it were. All businesses must, of course, react in the most suitable manner to external influences in order to survive, especially when these generate cash flow problems and similar critical situations, such as falling demand for products and services.

A business invariably belongs to a particular industry, i.e. car manufacture, automotive products, food, textiles, chemicals, engineering, package holidays (tour operators), banking, insurance, and so on. Such industries, and indeed the individual businesses comprising the industries, are essential elements in the national economic system. This system does not exist in isolation either, as it is an integral part of the world economic system, participating in world trade (in some instances) through imports and exports. Other types of business provide international insurance and financial services. Many businesses are, of course, multi-national companies, having overseas branches or factories.

The details which follow outline the economic environment applicable to most manufacturing businesses.

Clearly both national and international economic forces influence demand for the products of a particular business. This is especially so during periods of inflation, such as the present spiral from which the whole world is suffering. Spiralling prices on this scale greatly affect the purchasing power of individuals and businesses alike. The economic circumstances which prevail at present, and which, unfortunately, are likely to prevail in the future, must be taken into consideration when forecasting demand for a firm's products, as this is often the basis for establishing production programmes. The importance of demand depends upon whether a business produces standard products, for stock, or on the basis of specific orders from customers.

Production programmes, in turn, determine the resources required in the shape of raw materials and parts from the company's suppliers. The availability of these may, in turn, be influenced by strikes within the particular industry and by general world demand. The supply factor is also dependent upon the political, economic and social circumstances prevailing within the countries supplying basic raw materials such as oil, timber and copper, etc.

Demand naturally affects levels of employment; and levels of employment, both in this country and abroad, affect demand. For example, a high level of demand within our own national economy for capital goods creates additional demand, by those employed in capital goods industries, for consumer goods—

except in circumstances where demand is curtailed by inflation, or by government action to restrict demand.

Increasing demand for consumer goods at home creates additional demand for new plant and machinery, in order to expand production facilities. Unfortunately, such increased demand can create balance of payments problems in respect of raw materials and products purchased from other countries, which have to be financed by additional exports—the product of home-based factories.

On the other hand, a low level of employment reduces demand for consumer goods, and this causes firms to cut back their investment programmes. Such a cut-back reduces a company's ability to increase production quickly, should demand increase, as new plant and machinery may not be readily available at short notice. The suppliers of plant will also have reduced their production facilities in the interests of economy (*see* Fig. 2).

8. Technological environment. Very often, the technological developments of one industry generate technological spin-offs, which are adopted by other industries, notable examples being the development of electronics and control systems obtained from the results of space research. Consumers respond to such developments by requiring products incorporating the latest technology. A business must respond accordingly and develop products which are compatible with the latest developments. Examples of this include transistorised (solid state) radios and audio equipment; and the changeover to household products manufactured from plastics instead of metal. Only by this means may a business retain or increase its share of the market. This is where market research has an important part to play, as it is concerned with discovering consumer requirements. From this, sales forecasting attempts to define the likely level of demand for the products of the business.

Many large businesses conduct their own research, for eventual changeover to completely new products or redesigned products, to suit the needs of the market, providing they are economically viable. This is established from the results of conducting market research.

9. Financial environment. The effect of the present economic crisis is reflected in the financial position of many businesses as, in many cases, they are suffering from a deficiency of liquid financial resources with which to conduct business operations. This situation is largely attributable to falling demand, which decreases the revenue from which operating expenditure must be financed. One of the main factors is the fixed overheads of a business, which must be met regardless of the sales revenue achieved. In particular, a lower level of production increases the fixed cost per unit, which has the effect of reducing the profit margin on each unit sold. Even when a business can obtain short-term financial aid in the form of bank loans or overdrafts, the interest rate is quite high—which increases the financial overheads of the business.

10. Sociological environment. At the present time, employees are developing a new sociological outlook, as they are no longer content with being controlled in an autocratic manner, but prefer to participate in the management process in order to obtain a higher degree of job-enrichment. This requires management to alter their traditional attitude in the direction of a more democratic approach to business management.

11. Legislative environment. A great deal of government legislation, ranging from the Companies Acts to the Redundancy Payments Act, affects the conduct of business and, of course, business systems must incorporate the requirements of specific legislation. Some aspects of legislation place a considerable burden on a business, as many of these new activities are unproductive as far as the business is concerned. Instances of this type of legislation include VAT and PAYE, which require business systems to be geared up to deal with these procedures. Valuable resources are occupied on such tasks, which do not provide any financial returns or benefits of any kind to the business.

PROGRESS TEST 1

1. "Enlightened business managers have had the vision to see the need for business operations to be conducted within the framework of sophisticated 'space age' business systems." Discuss this statement indicating the important factors which make this necessary and the types of business system that should be considered. (1)

2. There exists a galaxy of business systems, each custom-built to suit the needs of individual businesses. Classify the types of business system which may need to be considered when assessing

the requirements of any particular business, indicating their main features and characteristics. (2, Table I)

3. "Whatever the nature of a system it is imperative that it should be dynamic or adaptive so that it can respond to change in a flexible manner." Discuss this statement. (2, 3)

4. What do you understand by the term "tuning business systems"? (3)

5. Indicate the need for co-operation and co-ordination between the physical operations of a business and the various business systems to which they are related. (4)

6. Business systems require resources to enable them to operate, in the same way that a factory requires resources. Indicate the types of resources required. (5)

7. No business exists in a vacuum and so cannot entirely control its own destiny, as it is subjected to external influences over which it has no direct control. Outline the environmental factors which influence the operations of a business. (6–11)

CHAPTER II

Purpose and Objectives of Business Systems

PURPOSE, OBJECTIVES AND MANAGEMENT OF CHANGE

1. Purpose and objective. The prime reason for the initial implementation of a system is because it is deemed to have a useful purpose. A system without a useful purpose should not remain in existence, as it employs resources which could be used to greater advantage in other operations of the business. A system, to serve a useful purpose, must be goal-orientated which means it must

TABLE II. PURPOSE AND OBJECTIVES OF BUSINESS SYSTEMS

System	Purpose	Objective
Stock control	To control stocks of materials and parts.	To control the level of stocks to avoid storage of excessive stocks but also to avoid excessive stock shortages and to optimise the cost of ordering and carrying stocks.
Wages	To compile employees earnings and prepare payslips, payrolls and tax and earnings records. Wages analysis.	To calculate and payout wages by a stated day and time. Cost control.
Purchasing	To obtain all types of materials, parts and equipment for the business.	To obtain supplies at the most economical prices, of the right quality at the right time.

have defined objectives. Such objectives must be within the framework of overall business objectives, as only by this means can it be ensured that all systems have a common aim. Table II will perhaps clarify the significance of purpose and objective.

2. Systems appraisal. A systems outlook, and a systematic appraisal of business systems, is essential for effective business operations, as systems often outlive their useful purpose. In such cases, a system must be modified or discontinued, in order to be compatible with current circumstances. A particular instance of this arose with the introduction of VAT, which affected the purchasing and sales systems of many businesses.

In other instances, the original purpose of a system may still be valid but, due to business growth, the sheer volume of data to be processed may necessitate a change of method. This might be, perhaps, from a clerical activity to a machine activity, which, at the present time, may be to a visible record computer (small office computer) or even a larger main frame computer. This is where administrative management have an important part to play (*see* 3).

3. Management of change. Administrative management must systematically appraise the activities of the departments for which they are accountable, since they need to be aware of the need for change as circumstances dictate. In this respect, all levels of administrative management, whether in charge of functions, departments or sections, should act as agents of change. Only by this means can a business react dynamically to changing situations and remain an effective unit within an industry and the national economy as a whole.

Responding to change at the right moment requires vision, which itself requires an analytical approach in an attempt to foresee events which will necessitate change to particular business systems. Managers need to adopt an outwards-looking, rather than a narrow, inwards-looking stance, so that they may have a panoramic view, instead of a mere foreground snapshot, of the business environment. Only by this means will they see the wood for the trees, and only in this way will business systems and equipment be upgraded on a planned basis, as changing circumstances require. Only in this way will the purpose and objectives of systems be redefined. The alternative is haphazard, "fire alarm" exercises which can only result in disruption, frustration, low productivity and overall inefficiency.

It was stated earlier (*see* I, **3**) that O. & M. investigators and systems analysts provide a valuable service to administrative management by enabling them to react to change, painlessly, in a relative sense. This is possible, because most of the investigatory and systems design activities are removed from the shoulders of administrative management as they are performed by O. & M. and systems staff.

Administrative management should, without doubt, participate in the bringing-about of changes they deem necessary because, after all, they are responsible for specific activities on a day-to-day basis and should be aware of situations which are developing and which require their attention. It must be appreciated that they are often pre-occupied with daily, routine problems and may not have time at their disposal for critical appraisal of the operations being performed. They should, however, obtain an appreciation of the situation by internal communication. Managers can then request assistance from the O. & M. and systems personnel.

PURPOSE—OTHER FACTORS

4. Interdependence of purpose of systems. Before production can commence in a manufacturing business it is necessary to forecast sales demand, which is an activity performed by the marketing (sales) function. From the forecast, the production planning system prepares production programmes and material and parts requirements. These requirements are adjusted by the existing stocks held in the stores and this involves the stock control system which supplies the stock figures. Raw materials and parts are then ordered and this is the concern of the purchasing system (buying office) which places orders with selected suppliers.

When supplies are received, they are routed either directly to the manufacturing processes (the factory system) or, which is more likely, to the stores. The stock control system becomes involved, since the items received need to be recorded on stock records to show the latest stock position. The accounting system is responsible for recording details of items sent direct to the factory on job cost records, but this depends upon the type of manufacture, because standard products utilise standard costs rather than job costs. The accounts of suppliers also need to be updated to record the value of items purchased from them, as shown on purchase invoices.

Subsequently, the purchasing system again comes on the scene:

it is responsible for authorising payment of suppliers' accounts which eventually brings the accounting system into the picture, as it makes the payments to suppliers.

The production planning system issues production orders to the production departments (factory system), including requisitions for materials and parts to be withdrawn from stores. When these orders are activated, the stock control system records the issues on the stock records and the accounting system records the cost of the issues on job cost records, when appropriate.

All employees, including factory operatives, administrative staff and managers must be remunerated for their labour and the accounting system calculates wages and salaries and prepares payslips and payrolls as well as other related records.

Completed production is despatched to the finished goods warehouse where the stock control system records the receipts on finished stock records. The production planning system also records the finished production on its production schedules for progressing purposes. When products are withdrawn from the stores and despatched to customers, the stock control system records the transactions on stock records to show the current stock position.

The sales system prepares invoices and the accounting system records the sales details on the appropriate customers' sales record. When remittances are received from customers, the accounting system records them on the appropriate sales records to show the current balances outstanding. Statements of account are prepared each month to inform customers of their outstanding balance for goods supplied (*see* Fig. 3).

5. Dual purpose systems. In many instances, business systems serve a dual purpose, since their purpose is not only to produce invoices, statements of account, payslips, issue notes, goods received notes and purchase orders, etc., but also to produce schedules in the form of analyses relating to wages, sales, profitability of products, purchases, expenditure and production, etc. In addition, various types of report are compiled, often in the form of Exception Reports, showing variances from planned results, i.e. cash flow statements, profit and loss statements, budget statements, stocks requiring replenishment and overdue accounts, etc. (*see* I, **5**(*d*)).

6. Early warning system. Exception reports in particular provide an early warning system of situations which are likely to have

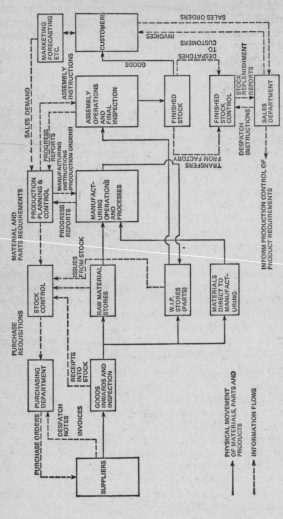

FIG. 3   Interaction of manufacturing and related systems.

adverse effects on the business. The early warning system sets off "alarm bells" in a time-scale relevant to the response-time needs of particular systems, so that appropriate defensive measures can be taken which may be either of a tactical or strategic nature.

7. Monitoring systems. The purpose of some systems is to monitor other systems (*see* I, **4** and XII). To monitor means to control, and a control system may be defined as a "control loop" superimposed on another system having a different purpose, e.g. the production system, which is controlled by the production-control system. Monitoring is for the purpose of detecting variations in the behaviour of a system, so that control signals can be communicated to the appropriate manager. He is then in a position to effect changes to the system he is managing, so that it reverts to the desired state and so achieves its objectives. Many administrative systems are control-orientated but they do not effect control directly—this is the prerogative of the manager concerned. Other control systems include stock control, cost control, budgetary control, quality control and credit control (*see* XI, **18–23**).

8. Planning systems. The purpose of some systems is to plan the operations of other systems, a notable example being the production planning system (often called production-control, but it embraces both planning and control elements) which is responsible for planning production programmes (*see* I, **4**). Planning is mainly concerned with the allocation of resources to specific tasks and the setting of performance targets. A plan establishes the guide lines for future action, without which a business is likely to drift in the wrong direction. Plans set a course for the business to follow guided by the navigator, usually the chief executive. Plans very often form the basis for preparing budgets.

In addition, it may be said that planning is concerned with:

(*a*) What is to be done.
(*b*) When it is to be done.
(*c*) Where it is to be done.
(*d*) Who is to do it.
(*e*) How it is to be done.
(*see* VIII, **6**).

HIERARCHY OF SYSTEM OBJECTIVES

9. Defining objectives. Business organisations have a hierarchy of management consisting of the board of directors, functional managers, departmental managers and section supervisors. As a business achieves its objective through the actions of managers, it follows that there should be a compatible hierarchy of system objectives, for the purpose of indicating to each manager the performance expected from him (*see* Table III).

TABLE III. HIERARCHY OF SYSTEM OBJECTIVES

Classification of objectives	Type of objective
Corporate	Strategic business objectives
System	Functional: operational and tactical objectives
Sub-system	Departmental: tactical objectives

10. Corporate objectives. Before a business is capable of defining the objectives of individual systems, it must specify and clarify its corporate objectives, which vary for different types of business, but for a manufacturing business they would probably include:

(a) Economic purpose of the business.
(b) Type of products to be marketed.
(c) Markets aimed at.
(d) Share of market required.
(e) Rate of growth required in respect of sales.
(f) Profit and return on capital.

To be able to do this, a business must first assess its strengths and weaknesses, together with constraints on any proposed courses of action. It is pointless planning an increase in sales beyond the production capacity available. Similarly, it is not practical to consider marketing a new product without the necessary skills and manufacturing resources.

11. System objectives. The term system, in the context of this book, is used to define all the procedures which support a functional activity such as marketing and production. System objectives therefore may be defined as those relating to specific business functions. They must be compatible with corporate objectives, as it is through the achievement of system objectives that a business achieves its overall aims.

Objectives should be specified in meaningful and unambiguous terms and this requires that they be stated *quantitatively*. Monitoring is then simplified, as the actual performance of a system can be more easily compared with its planned performance. For example, a factory may be required to increase its output of products by a stipulated percentage. This will be incorporated in the production plan prepared by the production planning and control department, which is responsible for planning and monitoring factory output. The factory management is responsible for achieving the planned output. The factory may also be required to reduce production costs by a stated percentage—which, again, is the responsibility of factory management. Monitoring cost-performance is the responsibility of the cost department through its cost-control systems.

12. Sub-system objectives. A sub-system may be defined as a departmental activity within the framework of a functional activity. Individual departments are set objectives within the framework of functional objectives and accordingly they may be defined as sub-objectives. The factory objective to reduce production costs may be achieved by a sub-analysis of factors which will achieve this requirement and accordingly sub-objectives may be as shown in Table IV.

TABLE IV. PRODUCTION DEPARTMENT SUB-OBJECTIVES

Sub-objective	*Monitored by:*
Increase machine utilisation by 5 per cent to 85 per cent	Factory management and Production planning and control
Reduce idle time from 2 per cent to 1 per cent of total production time	Factory management and Production planning and control
Reduce labour turnover from 15 per cent to 5 per cent	Factory management and Personnel department
Increase operator performance to an average of 120 per cent from present 110 per cent	Factory management and Work study department
Reduce scrapped output to 5 per cent of good production from present 8 per cent	Factory management and Quality control department

As a further example, Table V outlines the system objectives and sub-objectives of a sales department processing incoming customers' orders. It may be assumed that the control of finished stock is the responsibility of the sales department.

TABLE V. SALES DEPARTMENT OBJECTIVES AND SUB-OBJECTIVES

System objective	Sub-objective
Improve customer satisfaction	Reduce delivery time of orders by 5 days
	Ensure that special orders are notified to the product design office the day they are received
	Ensure that orders are acknowledged and delivery dates quoted within 2 days
	Improve accuracy of quoting delivery dates—margin of error must not exceed one week
Optimise stock levels	Minimise stock shortages by more sophisticated stock control and demand fore-casting techniques to 95 per cent confidence level
	Reduce average inventory by 10 per cent

The objectives indicated above form part of the overall marketing strategy, which may include objectives to increase the market share of defined products and their profitability. Product profitability is also dependent upon the factory objectives outlined in Table IV.

13. The influence of the human element on objectives. When management set business objectives they must never ignore the fact that people are involved in their achievement and very often organisational objectives may not correspond with the objectives of the personnel which form the organisation. A great deal depends upon the motivational influences which exist, if any, and their value to individuals. Incentive schemes are often linked to objectives as a motivating influence but, even so, targets may be set at a level which personnel consider too high, regardless of the monetary inducement which may be available. Other motivating elements may be considered, such as a greater participation in decision-making in order to stimulate job interest, but even this will cause varying reactions from individuals. Some personnel may require a less demanding working environment, increased leisure-time, more welfare facilities or, perhaps, more status. These are socio-technical factors, involving consideration of social sciences with respect to the behavioural aspects of people at work.

With automated systems, it is possible to predict what outputs will be achieved from specified inputs, but such systems require programming and people are not susceptible to being programmed as automatons. Perhaps the answer lies in the area of effective leadership, fair dealing, good communications and recognising that people are human beings.

PROGRESS TEST 2

1. "Systems must serve a useful purpose and have defined objectives." Discuss this statement.   (1, Table II)

2. Discuss the general objectives of administrative systems and show the common characteristics that such systems should have.
(1)   (I.A.M. S1975, Paper A, Q1)

3. Systems may need to be modified or discontinued in order to be compatible with current circumstances. Indicate circumstances when this may apply.   (2)

4. What is an "agent of change"? How might an Office Manager perform this function?   (3)

(I.A.M. S1973, Paper No. 2, Q1)

5. The administrator needs to be sensitive and responsive to the need for change. How can this sensitivity and responsiveness be adequately developed?   (3)

(I.A.M. W1973, Paper No. 2, Q1)

6. Since many systems have evolved over a period of time, the objectives of such systems have often become clouded. Would a periodic redefinition of objectives, necessitating commensurate redesign, be justified, bearing in mind the resultant design and training effort involved and the inevitable upheaval?   (3)

(I.A.M. W1973, Paper No. 1, Q6)

7. How does the administrative manager recognise the need for change and ensure that change is neither premature, nor overdue? (3)   (I.A.M. S1975, Paper B, Q1)

8. Outline the interdependence of purpose of the systems which comprise a typical manufacturing business. (4)

9. In many instances, business systems serve a dual purpose as they produce output in addition to basic business documents. Indicate the form other types of output are likely to take. (5)

10. Exception reports provide an early warning system of situations likely to have adverse effects on the business. How is this achieved? (6)

11. What is the relative importance of monitoring compared with other steps in the systems cycle and how may it be performed effectively? (7)   (I.A.M. W1973, Paper No. 2, Q2)

12. The purpose of some systems is to plan the operations of other systems. What are the main activities concerned with planning? (8)

13. Business organisations operate on the basis of a hierarchy of objectives. What is the purpose of this structure of objectives and how may they be classified? (9–12, Tables III–V)

14. As well as providing information, systems have significant effect on people, their attitudes, and their motivation. Discuss this statement and suggest how dysfunctional effects can be avoided. (13)   (I.A.M. S1974, Part A, Q3)

CHAPTER III

The Nature of Non-Financial Systems

BASIC CONSIDERATIONS

1. Definition of non-financial system. The term non-financial system is used to define those systems having a main purpose other than of a financial nature. Some systems in this category do, however, have financial implications, i.e. the purchasing system is predominantly concerned with ordering materials and parts required for manufacturing and other purposes, but the system also authorises payments to suppliers for goods received from them. This of course is a financial matter. After payments are authorised the accounting system, responsible for financial aspects of transactions, makes the payments to suppliers. Similarly, the sales system is concerned with processing customers' orders and despatching goods, but accounts of customers and their remittances are administered by the accounting system.

2. Suites of related procedures. Although separate procedures exist for specific routines, a system may consist of several related procedures—a suite of procedures—but all such procedures may not be carried out by one function as evidenced above. This arises partly for specialisation and administrative convenience, but also for the application of internal check procedures. Internal check procedures are formulated on the principle that systems dealing with non-financial activities should be distinct from the financial aspects (accounting aspects) associated with such activities. This is mainly as a safeguard to prevent collusion to perpetrate fraud (*see* XII, **11**).

When a computer is used for processing data, it is often used as a service for the whole of a business and, in such instances, what were originally separate procedures performed in different functions, become an integrated suite of programs.

This recognises the close relationships which some systems or procedures possess, particularly as the output from some are the input to others (*see* VI, **1**).

As the main purpose of this book is a "systems view" of business systems, analytical aspects will be dealt with in X and XI.

Accordingly, the system outlines which follow will be restricted to their main characteristics.

THE PURCHASING SYSTEM

3. Purpose. The purpose of the purchasing system is to obtain all types of materials, parts and equipment for the business (*see* Table II). This may be expanded to include the preparation of purchase orders for such supplies and the progressing of orders, to ensure that supplies are received as near as possible to the stated delivery date.

4. Principles. The principles indicate the framework of policy in which the activity should be conducted and includes the following factors:

(*a*) Purchase requisitions should be checked to ensure that they are originated by authorised personnel.

(*b*) Purchase requisitions should be edited for correctness of item description and specification.

(*c*) Orders for supplies by telephone should be verified by an official order form.

5. Objectives. The objectives indicate the goals to be attained which, in this instance, are to obtain supplies at the most economic price consistent with the quality required and to ensure they are received at the right time (*see* Table II).

6. Basic purchasing activities. The main activities are concerned with processing purchase requisitions, determining sources of supply and arranging acceptable terms for price (including quantity discounts when appropriate), quality and delivery. Such activities may be analysed into three basic procedures as follows:

(*a*) Purchase order procedure (*see* Fig. 4).

(*b*) Goods receiving procedure (*see* Fig. 5).

(*c*) Authorisation for payment procedure (*see* Fig. 6).

The purchasing system is very often responsible for controlling stocks, but this system is outlined separately in a later section of this chapter (*see* **8–12**).

7. Other purchasing activities. Apart from the main activities outlined above, the purchasing system performs additional important functions which are summarised as follows.

(*a*) Ensuring that forward orders are placed in sufficient time to meet production schedules.

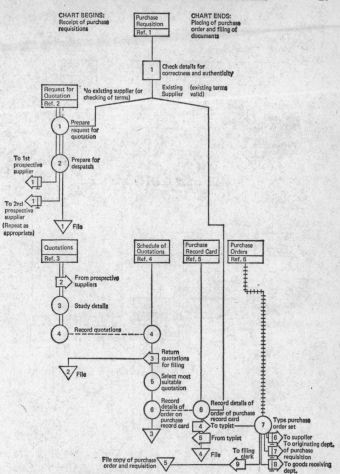

FIG. 4   *Procedure chart. Purchase order procedure.*

(b) Ensuring that standard prices are obtained as far as market conditions allow.

(c) Determining the Economic Order Quantity (EOQ) for each stock item purchased in conjunction with stock controller and management accountant.

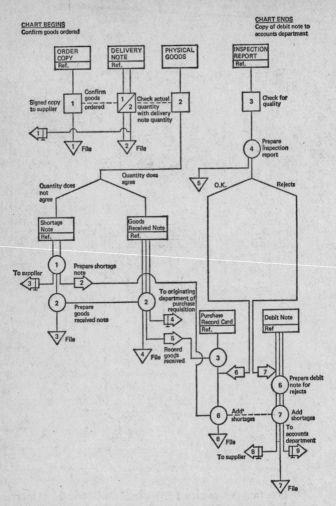

FIG. 5   *Procedure chart. Goods receiving procedure.*

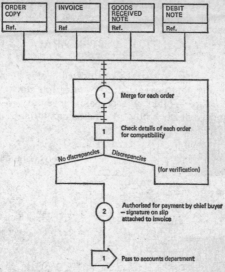

FIG. 6 *Procedure chart. Authorisation for payment procedure.*

(*d*) Establishing stock control levels: minimum, maximum, and re-order level, in accordance with "lead time" (*see* **12**(*c*)) and safety stock factors, to avoid stock shortages on the one hand and excessive stocks on the other. This procedure is necessary for each stock item purchased. The levels are determined in conjunction with the stock controller and are revised, as appropriate, to contend with changing circumstances.

(*e*) Rationalising range of materials purchased, in conjunction with Material Controller.

(*f*) Progressing orders to ensure that deliveries from suppliers attain scheduled dates as far as possible.

(*g*) Providing reports in respect of price changes to Management Accountant.

(*h*) Providing reports to Production Manager and Production Controller in respect of changes in the supply position.

(*i*) Providing reports on new materials to Chief Product Designer and Material Controller.

(*j*) Providing standard price schedules to Management Accountant.

(k) Checking incoming purchase invoices for accuracy.

(l) Authorising payment for purchases.

THE STOCK CONTROL SYSTEM—RAW MATERIALS AND PARTS

8. Purpose. The main purpose of stock control is the monitoring of stock levels and this is achieved by recording stock movements on stock records—often on a perpetual inventory basis. By this means the current stock situation, including shortages, is available (*see* Fig. 7).

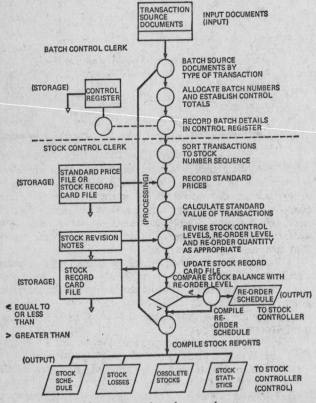

FIG. 7   *Outline of stock control system.*

9. Principles. The principles governing the administration of stock control are as follows:

(a) Stock transactions must be supported by authorised documentation.

(b) Stock movements should be recorded as documents are received, without unnecessary delay.

(c) Stock movements should be recorded with accuracy.

(d) Amended stock control parameters should be recorded on relevant stock records before processing transactions, so that any action taken relates to current circumstances. This is particularly important when re-order levels are adjusted (see 12(a)).

10. Objectives. It must be appreciated that stocks form a buffer to facilitate variations in supply and demand and, as they are often a high proportion of working capital, they must be controlled in the most effective manner to achieve the following (see Table II).

(a) Avoidance of excessive stocks.

(b) Avoidance of excessive stock shortages.

(c) Optimise cost of ordering supplies.

(d) Optimise cost of carrying stocks.

11. Other stock control activities. One important activity is to achieve a high degree of co-ordination with the purchasing system, by ensuring that stock items are replenished in accordance with the pre-determined re-order level and Economic Order Quantity, established in conjunction with purchasing personnel. Other activities include:

(a) The provision of reports in respect of stock losses, shortages, dormant, obsolete and free stocks, to Production Controller.

(b) The provision of schedules in respect of issues to production and stock balances—quantity and value—to the Management Accountant for the preparation of periodic operating reports and balance sheets.

12. Stock control parameters. The control of stocks is achieved not only by recording stock movements, but also by means of control parameters for each item of stock. Examples of such parameters are:

(a) *Re-order level.* The level of stock which signifies that it is necessary to place an order to replenish stocks.

(b) *Economic Order Quantity.* The Economic Order Quantity is calculated by balancing two opposing costs—stock-holding costs which increase as the order size (quantity) increases and ordering (purchasing) costs which decrease as the order size increases. When both costs are equal, the total costs (stock-holding costs and ordering costs) are at a minimum.

(c) *Safety stock*. The quantity of items which provide a buffer against variations in lead time (the number of days or weeks which elapse from the point of placing an order to receiving the goods ordered) and usage during lead time.

(d) *Maximum stock*. The quantity of stock which should not be exceeded, except in special circumstances, to avoid both storage problems and over-investment in stocks.

(e) *Average stock*. The average investment in stock is a useful parameter for indicating to management the extent to which the actual investment on average has fluctuated from the target.

THE MARKETING SYSTEM

13. Introduction. It is not the intention to deal with the marketing function in depth, as the primary purpose of this chapter is outlining the main characteristics of typical business systems. However, before indicating the characteristics of a sales system, a sub-system within the marketing function, it is deemed appropriate to indicate the framework of the marketing function, for orientation purposes.

14. Purpose. The marketing function is primarily concerned with product/market development, taking into account product life-cycles, competition, trend of demand, changing market needs, share of market required and the economic environment (*see* I, 7). Having defined and developed markets, the function is then actively concerned with selling to customers, supported by administrative procedures which are to be outlined (*see* **19–23**).

15. Principles. The framework of policy in which the marketing function operates may be defined as follows:

(a) Contribute to the economic needs of the community by supplying the goods and services it needs.

(b) Contribute to the economic and social well-being of the community by improving products when possible and ensuring that they have the highest functional performance, consistent with price. This also implies that the products and services should have a high safety factor.

(*c*) Ensuring that certain products do not become freely available to specific sections of the public, e.g. for young people, cigarettes, alcohol, fireworks and dangerous chemicals.

(*d*) To pass on price reductions whenever possible. Such reductions these days are of course the exception, rather than the rule, in the present inflationary economy. The government controls prices in many cases by the provision of subsidies to manufacturers, for the purpose of avoiding price increases which the manufacturer would otherwise have to pass on to the consumer.

16. Objectives. The main objective is to narrow or eliminate the strategic gap which separates likely achievements, based on forecasts, from what the board of directors wants to achieve, in respect of market share, growth, profit and return on capital. The strategy to achieve this objective varies with circumstances, but is mainly concerned with product/market development and the factors outlined in **14,** above.

17. Main functions. These may be summarised as follows (*see* Fig. 8).

    (*a*) Product development.
    (*b*) Market research.
    (*c*) Sales forecasting.
    (*d*) Sales promotion.
    (*e*) Selling.
    (*f*) Sales administration:
      (*i*) Sales procedures.
      (*ii*) Control of finished stock.
    (*g*) Distribution.
    (*h*) After-sales service.

18. Basic marketing activities. The broad activities are concerned with marketing strategy, selling, distribution and sales administration. Such activities may be summarised as follows:

(*a*) Planning marketing strategy.

(*b*) Ensuring that orders are suitably edited and customers scrutinised for credit status.

(*c*) Controlling finished stocks to achieve an acceptable level of customer service, whilst maintaining the average inventory as low as possible.

(*d*) Monitoring and analysing complaints from customers.

(*e*) Controlling product profitability by liaison with the Management Accountant.

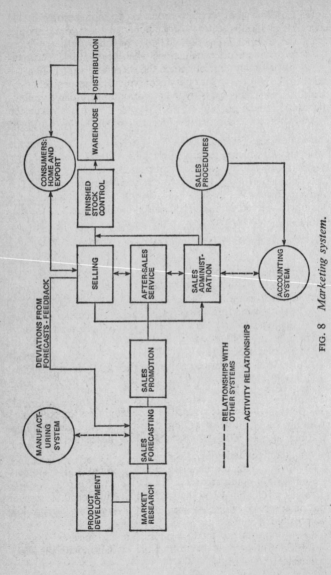

FIG. 8 *Marketing system.*

(*f*) Controlling achievements of salesmen by comparing actual results with targets.

(*g*) Monitoring the effectiveness of advertising media.

(*h*) Controlling marketing costs by liaison with the Management Accountant, by means of budgetary control.

THE SALES SYSTEM

19. Introduction. The sales system to be described is a sub-system within the marketing system, dealing with customers' orders. The customers' requirements are supplied from stock, referred to as "goods ex-stock", and invoices are prepared from priced and extended copies of despatch notes. Invoices are prepared after the goods have been despatched to customers and this is referred to as "post invoicing". In some systems, invoices and despatch documentation are prepared as a multi-part set on receipt of orders from customers. This is referred to as "pre-invoicing", as invoices are prepared before despatch of goods to customers (*see* Fig. 9).

20. Purpose. To deal with customers' orders and their acknowledgment, preparation of despatch documentation, monitoring stock shortages and invoicing goods to customers. Very often, sales orders are received by telephone and the manner in which enquiries and discussions are dealt with reflects the image of the business. Apart from the salesmen in the field, telephone conversations with customers by sales office staff also provide a link between the external and internal business environment. The telephone system in this case becomes a system interface, as it serves the purpose of linking systems together (*see* VI, **2**).

21. Principles. The principles on which the sales system should run may be summarised as follows:

(*a*) All communications with customers should be conducted with courtesy.

(*b*) Ensuring that orders are edited before being processed, so that catalogue or product numbers and quantities are correct.

(*c*) Ensuring that delivery dates are accurately quoted by checking the stock position first.

(*d*) Ensuring that the credit status of customers is checked and proved satisfactory before acceptance of orders.

22. Objectives. As the sales system deals with customers, the principle objective must be to improve customer satisfaction, and

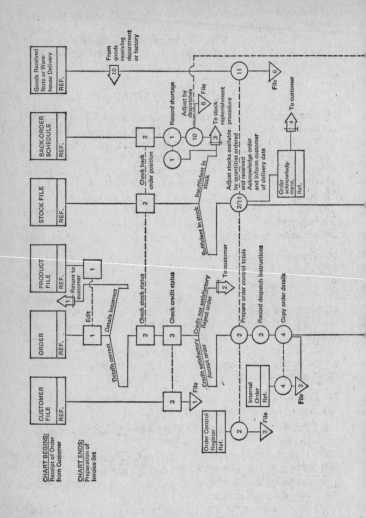

CHART BEGINS:
Receipt of Order
from Customer

CHART ENDS:
Preparation of
Invoice Set

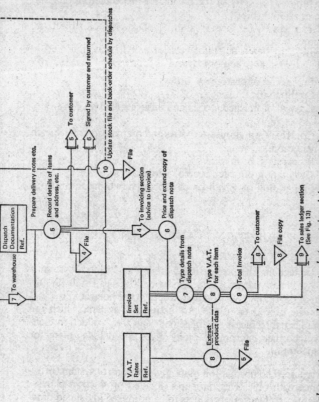

FIG. 9   *Sales system—goods ex-stock (post invoicing system) (order to invoicing).*

customers tell suppliers how this may be done in no uncertain terms. It is *essential* to take heed of a customer's requirements, as the future prosperity of the business is dependent upon good customer relationships.

Refer to Table V for further examples of sales system objectives.

23. Sales activities. The framework of activities is indicated in Fig. 9 and these may be summarised as follows:

(*a*) Processing of customers' orders.

(*b*) Credit control.

(*c*) Control of finished stocks and ensuring that stocks are replenished as appropriate.

(*d*) Control of warehouse activities and preparation of dispatch documentation.

(*e*) Preparation of invoices.

(*f*) Calculation of order control totals.

(*g*) Preparation of schedules of shortages relating to previous orders.

THE PRODUCTION PLANNING AND CONTROL SYSTEM

24. Introduction. The production planning and control system is a sub-system of the production system, which is, itself, a sub-system of the business as a complete entity. The board of directors defines the objectives of the production sub-system, which are communicated to factory management and the Production Controller, who then interprets the objectives into detailed plans for implementation.

25. Purpose. The production planning and control system, in accordance with objectives, prepares detailed production plans—the quantities of various products to be produced in defined time-periods—which stipulate *what* has to be done and *when*, the resources required and the methods to be employed. It is also responsible for organising the flow of materials and parts required for the production programmes, after consideration of scrap allowances, stock policy and the existing stock of materials and parts. Detailed programmes are also prepared for shop and machine loading. Imbalance may occur between different processes and rescheduling may be required to optimise the use of resources. Appropriate action also needs to be taken for excessive spare capacity on the one hand, or insufficient capacity on the other. The system is also responsible for issuing works-order documentation and monitoring production operations (*see* Figs. 10 and 11).

26. Principles. The underlying principles with which the production planning and control system is concerned are as follows:

(*a*) Ensuring that production delays are kept to a minimum by prompt action to remove the cause of such delays.

(*b*) Ensuring that details of completed production are communicated without delay, to enable schedules to be updated in the shortest possible time, so that the current status of production is apparent.

(*c*) Ensuring that control reports are communicated to factory and production management within a prescribed time-scale.

27. Objectives. The main objectives may be said to be to keep production rolling to maintain output targets, within quality and cost constraints. Other objectives outlined in Table IV are:

(*a*) Increase machine utilisation by a stated percentage.

(*b*) Increase manpower utilisation by a stated percentage.

(*c*) Ensuring that arrears of production are cleared within a stipulated time.

28. Production planning and control activities. The framework of activities are outlined in Figs. 10 and 11 and may be summarised as follows:

(*a*) Production planning and programming.

(*b*) Material and parts planning.

(*c*) Controlling quantities manufactured for stock by the establishment of Economic Batch Quantities (EBQ) in conjunction with Management Accountant.

(*d*) Make-or-buy decisions, in consultation with the buying office (purchasing system) and Management Accountant.

(*e*) Issuing works-order documentation to manufacturing departments, including operation job cards, material requisitions, progress tickets, route cards, and inspection tickets.

(*f*) Controlling production by investigating and reporting on production delays, indicating causes, i.e. late delivery of materials, plant breakdown, power failure, excessive scrap, errors in production drawings and excessive absenteeism, etc.

(*g*) Updating schedules on receipt of progress tickets indicating the completion of operations and processes.

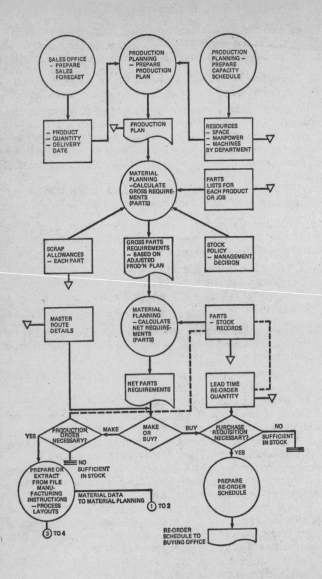

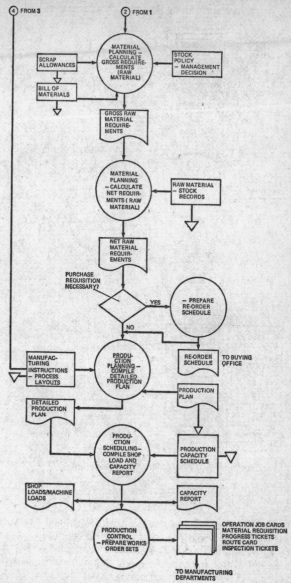

FIG. 10 *Production planning and scheduling procedure.*

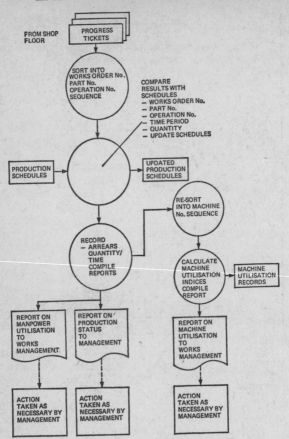

FIG. 11   *Production control (reporting and labour control elements only).*

(*h*) Comparing actual achievements with scheduled targets and noting significant deviations for management action.

(*i*) Providing factory and production management with performance statistics, indicating manpower and machine utilisation and reports in respect of arrears and material shortages.

PROGRESS TEST 3

1. Some systems are of a non-financial nature yet have financial implications. Indicate why this is so.   (1)

2. Although separate procedures exist for specific routines, a system may consist of several related procedures which may not be carried out by the same function. Explain the reasons for this. (2)

3. Indicate the purpose of a purchasing system and state the principles by which it is conducted, its objectives and activities. (3–7)

4. Prepare a systems flowchart for a typical manual purchasing system of a manufacturing organisation, from the time of the requisitioning of material by stores to the time of payment of the supplier's account.   (6, Figs. 4–6; IV, 7, 8, Fig. 14)

(I.A.M. S1973, Paper No. 2, Q2)

5. Indicate the purpose of a stock control system, in respect of raw materials and parts, and state the principles by which it is conducted, its objectives and activities.   (8–11)

6. The control of stocks is achieved not only by recording stock movements but also by control parameters. Give examples of relevant parameters.   (12)

7. Indicate the purpose of a marketing system stating the principles by which it is conducted, its objectives and functions and activities.   (13–18)

8. A sales system is a sub-system of the marketing system which administers customers' orders. Indicate its purpose, the principles by which it is conducted, its objectives and activities. (19–23)

9. The production planning and control system is a sub-system of the production system. Indicate its purpose, the principles by which it is conducted, its objectives and activities.   (24–8)

CHAPTER IV

The Nature of Financial Systems

FUNCTIONS OF FINANCIAL ACCOUNTING SYSTEMS

1. Definition of financial systems. These systems are primarily concerned with recording business transactions in respect of wages and salaries, purchases, sales and other aspects of income and expenditure, both capital and revenue. Records of such transactions provide the basis for the preparation of periodic or annual profit and loss accounts and balance sheets.

As can be seen, the financial systems of a business are, effectively, accounting systems which are often structured as separate systems to the non-financial systems (*see* III). When systems are computerised, the separately structured systems are often integrated, for economy of data processing and administrative efficiency. Systems integration is discussed in VI.

At this juncture, it will facilitate the reader's understanding of the nature of financial systems if a broad backcloth is portrayed of their functions.

2. Primary functions of financial systems. The primary functions to be outlined indicate the general principles which are applied to the administration of financial systems. One of the most important principles is to ensure that all business transactions are recorded in proper books of account, on the basis of recognised accounting practice. Such accounting transactions are largely for purposes of custodianship, as a public limited company is responsible to the shareholders—the owners of the business—and accordingly it is essential that the business records portray a true and accurate record of profits and losses, assets and liabilities.

Other functions of financial systems are summarised below:

(*a*) Planning and controlling all expenditure, both capital and revenue.

(*b*) Controlling the receipt and payment of cheques, etc. relating to business transactions and the relevant banking transactions.

(*c*) Ensuring that statutory records are maintained in respect of VAT, PAYE, National Insurance and graduated pensions, etc.

(*d*) Safeguarding the assets of the business in respect of plant and machinery, stocks, debtors and cash.

(*e*) Implementing internal check procedures by organising office activities, so that no one person is responsible for completing transactions, thereby preventing fraudulent conversion since this may only be accomplished by collusion of several members of the staff. Internal check techniques also incorporate independent check figures and pre-lists, which are used for comparing the value of transactions posted with the value which should have been posted (*see* XII, **11**).

(*f*) Preparation and distribution of periodic and annual reports and statistics for internal control and statutory requirements.

3. The nominal ledger. The focal point of financial accounting systems is the nominal ledger, sometimes referred to as the general ledger. The nominal ledger consists of accounts in which transactions are recorded from the point of view of the business and these are classified as "impersonal accounts". Impersonal accounts are sub-divided into "real accounts" and "nominal accounts".

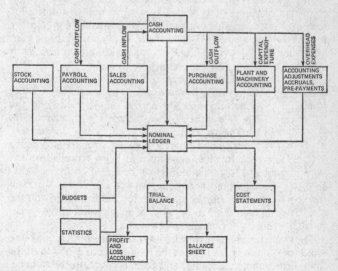

FIG. 12   *The nominal ledger.*

Real accounts are concerned with tangible assets such as plant, machinery and buildings, whereas nominal accounts are concerned with expenses, income, profits and losses. Financial accounting sub-systems are directly related to the nominal ledger by way of the double-entry convention for recording of business transactions. In respect of the Purchase accounting system, the nominal ledger contains the Purchase ledger control account and accounts for different classes of purchases. The Sales accounting system has accounts in the nominal ledger by way of the Sales ledger control account and the Sales account. Similarly, the Wages and salaries accounting system has the Wages and salaries control account and the Wages and salaries account in the nominal ledger.

Cash transactions, in respect of the sub-systems indicated above, are effected in the nominal ledger: for cash receipts from customers, they are recorded in the Bank account and the Sales ledger control account (*see* Fig. 12 and VI, **9**).

SALES ACCOUNTING SYSTEM

4. Invoicing and the sales ledger. The focal point of the Sales accounting system is the sales ledger, which is a subsidiary ledger consisting of records (accounts), relating to each customer, for recording sales supplied to them on credit. Invoices compiled by the Sales system (*see* III, **19–23** and Fig. 9) are posted to the sales ledger and the sales value is added to the outstanding balance, to indicate the amount owing on each account (*see* Fig. 13). It is important to appreciate however that a manual or mechanised accounting system would probably adopt a three-in-one writing technique, whereby invoices are posted simultaneously to the ledger card of the relevant customer, the posting summary (sales journal) and statement. This technique eliminates unnecessary duplication of entries and possible copying errors. Referring to Fig. 13, however, invoices are shown as being recorded on the sales journal and from the journal to the ledger accounts, as no specific method was meant to be shown in this instance. When all invoices have been recorded, the sales journal is totalled and the total is compared with the pre-list of invoice values to ensure posting errors do not remain undetected.

The posting summary, or sales journal, is, in effect, a day book which records daily credit sales the total of which is posted to the Sales ledger control account, and Sales account, in the nominal ledger, following the principles of double-entry accounting. The

Sales ledger control account records a credit balance which is the total of the individual balances on each sales account in the Sales ledger.

Invoices are also analysed for the purpose of compiling a VAT schedule and Product profitability report for management control. Account balances on the individual ledger accounts are also ana-

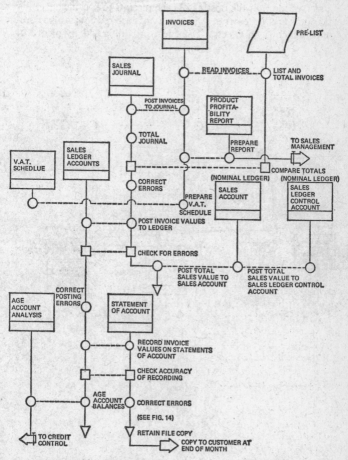

FIG. 13 *Invoices and sales accounting system.*

B.S.—4

lysed for the purpose of compiling an Account Age analysis, indicating the portion of the balance outstanding for one month, two months, three months and over three months. This is for credit control requirements, to detect accounts which have exceeded the credit period.

5. Cash receipts and the sales ledger. The sales ledger procedure also incorporates the posting of cash receipts to specific customer accounts and statements. A summary of cash receipts is also compiled which is, in effect, a Bank list, providing a daily record of

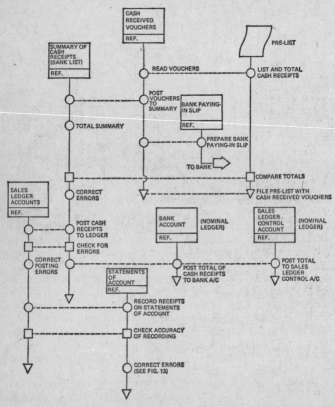

FIG. 14   *Cash receipts and sales accounting system.*

cash receipts. The total of the Bank list is posted to the Bank account and Sales ledger control account in the nominal ledger, following the convention of double-entry accounting (*see* Fig. 14). Ledger balances are reduced by cash receipts as they are by other types of adjustment such as returns from customers and invoice corrections.

6. Statements of account. Statements are despatched to customers at the end of each accounting period, which is normally each month. This is for the purpose of indicating to customers the state of their account for remittance purposes. After reconciling the amount owing from their own accounting records, customers remit part, or the whole, of the amount owing.

Balance-forward statements do not itemise the invoices or other debits constituting the opening balance, which is often the cause of customer queries and delays in payment. On the other hand, open item statements set out all debits and credits and show how cash receipts have been allocated so that the customer can more speedily reconcile the amount outstanding and reduce any delay in payment.

PURCHASE ACCOUNTING SYSTEM

7. Purchase invoices and the purchase ledger. The focal point of the Purchasing system is the purchase ledger, which is a subsidiary ledger consisting of records (accounts) relating to each supplier for recording purchases from them on credit. The threshold of the Purchase accounting system is the point when purchase invoices are received initially from the purchasing system, after they have been checked for accuracy of extensions. A check is also made to ensure that the goods have in fact been received and that official orders had been placed (*see* III, 3–7).

The invoices are recorded in the Purchase accounting system's Purchase journal which provides a daily record of purchases. The total of the purchase journal is posted to the Purchase ledger control account and to individual purchases accounts analysed to expense code in the nominal ledger. The invoices indicate expense codes by means of a slip attached to them.

Suppliers accounts are posted either from invoices or the purchase journal. The value of purchases from individual suppliers is added to the outstanding balance which indicates the amount owing to them (*see* Fig. 15). A VAT schedule is also compiled in respect of tax on each invoice.

Invoices are then returned to the purchasing system for further processing.

8. Cash payments and the purchase ledger. The purchasing system is responsible for authorising payments for purchases and the accounting system receives sets of documents comprising an order copy, invoice, goods received note and debit note for goods returned when appropriate (*see* Figs. 6 and 15).

The slip attached to the invoice is signed by a purchasing official, authorising payment. A remittance advice note and cheque, or traders credit transfer, are prepared and these are despatched to

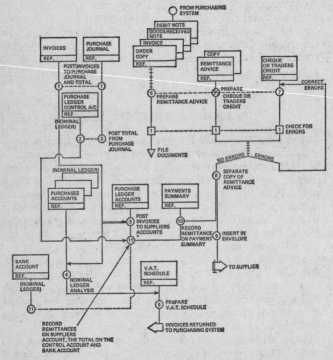

FIG. 15 *Purchase accounting system.*

the supplier. The remittances are recorded on a payments summary providing a daily record of cash payments. The total of the payments summary is debited to the Purchase ledger control account and credited to the Bank account, to complete the double entry in the nominal ledger. The accounts of suppliers are debited with remittances they have received, thereby reducing the balance owing to them.

In manual or mechanised purchase accounting systems, the three-in-one writing technique is often used for recording invoices on suppliers' accounts, purchase journal and the preparation of a remittance advice. Similarly, a purchase payment is recorded on a cheque or credit transfer, cash payments summary and the supplier's account.

FACTORY PAYROLL SYSTEM

9. Wages accounting. Although the details to be outlined relate to a factory payroll, similar considerations apply in respect of administrative and clerical staff who are paid a weekly or monthly salary. The main difference is in the manner of calculating the gross pay which, in the case of weekly and monthly paid personnel, is a fixed amount for the relevant period of time. With regard to factory operatives the method of calculating gross pay is dependent upon the type(s) of remuneration scheme in operation. This may be on the basis of attended hours, piece-work or bonus schemes.

Factory wages are normally paid a week in arrear, to allow sufficient time for the wages office to process the wages data received from the factory departments, in respect of the previous week. Typically, the data received from the factory includes clock cards, piecework tickets, job tickets, overtime authorisations and idle time cards. In addition, information on adjustments to pay rates, new starters and leavers is supplied by the personnel department.

The main record in the wages accounting system is the earnings and tax record of each employee, which is updated each pay period to show cumulative earnings and tax to date. When employees leave, a form indicating their tax and earnings to date is given to them for presentation to their new employer. The form is referred to as a P45 and it enables the new employer to record the details on an earnings and tax record. When posting each employee's

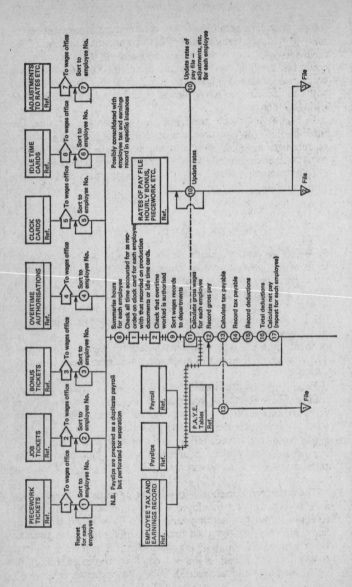

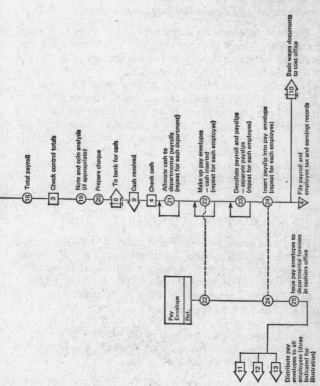

FIG. 16 Factory payroll system.

earnings and tax record, it is normal practice, when using writing boards or accounting machines, to simultaneously prepare the payroll and a payslip for each employee by the three-in-one technique.

In effect, the payroll is a posting summary and the relevant column totals are posted to appropriate accounts in the nominal ledger, e.g. gross wages, national insurance, standard deductions, income tax and superannuation, etc. (*see* Fig. 16).

A statement is issued to each employee at the end of each tax year with regard to earnings and tax; this is known as a P60.

10. Checks and controls. An important check to apply to the payroll is to ensure that it does not include fictitious employees, and this may be facilitated by a comparison of the names on the payroll with the file of National Insurance cards. Names without a corresponding National Insurance card may be subjected to further investigation to establish the reason. It may simply mean that cards have been taken out of the file for some reason.

It is essential to ensure that all adjustments to pay rates are supported by an authorising signature on a standard type of document. Similarly, payments for overtime and quantities produced, on the basis of a payments by results scheme, must also be authorised by appropriate officials.

FIXED ASSETS ACCOUNTING SYSTEM

11. Fixed asset accounting. The original cost of each type of fixed asset whether land, buildings or plant and machinery, is recorded in the appropriate account in the nominal ledger. In addition, the total annual depreciation for each type of asset is recorded (credited) in the depreciation provision account in the nominal ledger and the corresponding amount is debited to the profit and loss account.

For each type of asset, the total of the original costs and the respective depreciation provisions are recorded on the balance sheet so as to indicate the net book value.

12. The Plant and machinery register. The Plant and machinery register consists of records relating to fixed assets. Each item of plant and machinery has a separate record which is very often stored in a loose-leaf ledger or register. Such records serve a dual purpose, as follows:

(*a*) General information in respect of the item of plant or machine:

(*i*) Type of asset.
(*ii*) Supplier.
(*iii*) Manufacturer.
(*iv*) Description of asset.
(*v*) Horsepower or other power rating.
(*vi*) Floor area occupied.
(*vii*) Date of installation.
(*viii*) Location and transfers.

(*b*) A record for accounting control:

(*i*) Date of purchase.
(*ii*) Original cost.
(*iii*) Installation cost.
(*iv*) Depreciation class.
(*v*) Annual amount of depreciation.
(*vi*) Cumulative depreciation.
(*vii*) Written-down value.
(*viii*) Maintenance costs.
(*ix*) Cost of additions.
(*x*) Amount realised on disposal.

PROGRESS TEST 4

1. Indicate the primary functions of financial systems. **(1, 2)**
2. The focal point of financial accounting systems is the nominal ledger. Indicate in what ways the nominal ledger is related to financial accounting sub-systems. **(3)**
3. Outline the main features of a sales accounting system specifying the difference between "balance forward statements" and "open item statements". **(4–6)**
4. Outline the main features of a purchase accounting system. **(7, 8)**
5. Outline the main features of a factory payroll system indicating checks and controls that may be incorporated. **(9, 10)**
6. Outline the main features of a fixed assets accounting system specifying the contents and purposes of the Plant and machinery register. **(11, 12)**

CHAPTER V

The Nature of Management Accounting Systems

FUNCTIONS OF MANAGEMENT ACCOUNTING SYSTEMS

1. Management accounting. Most financial accounting systems extend into the realm of management accounting systems, which are for the purpose of ensuring that managers are supplied with information to guide them in achieving their objectives, in respect of the activities for which they are accountable. The broad scope of management accounting may be summarised as follows:

(*a*) Planning and controlling all cost and budgetary control procedures and systems.

(*b*) Preparation of periodic operating control statements showing the current and cumulative position of each budget centre and the business as a whole.

(*c*) Monitoring variances disclosed in operating statements and establishing the cause of such variances, for dissemination to operating managers and supervisors, to guide them in applying corrective action.

(*d*) Provision of cost and financial statistics and ratios for the board of directors.

(*e*) Preparation of cash flow statements indicating the source of funds and their disposition.

(*f*) Preparation of periodic profit and loss accounts and balance sheets.

(*g*) Preparation of standard product costs and their systematic revision.

(*h*) Preparation of product profitability reports on the basis of marginal costing and discounted cash flow techniques.

(*i*) Provision of information to facilitate "make-or-buy" decisions and for establishing economic manufacturing batch quantities.

(*j*) Provision of information for establishing economic order quantities.

(k) Provision of cost data for the preparation of product cost estimates.

2. Relationship of financial and management accounting systems. It is important to appreciate the interrelationships which exist between financial and management accounting systems and Table VI is meant to serve as a guide to such relationships. Clear demarcation lines are sometimes difficult to define in practice as they differ between businesses to provide for specific circumstances. Nevertheless, it is hoped Table VI will indicate the basic relationships.

TABLE VI. RELATIONSHIPS OF FINANCIAL AND MANAGEMENT
ACCOUNTING SYSTEMS

Financial accounting systems	Management accounting systems
1. Posting sales invoices to sales ledger	Sales variances from budget
2. Posting purchase invoices to purchase ledger	Purchase analysis and expenditure variances from budget
3. Preparation of payrolls	Wages and salaries analysis, variance analysis and control ratios
4. Posting Bank and cash transactions	Analysis of bank and petty cash payments for expenditure control and cash flow statements
5. Posting new acquisitions and disposals to Plant and machinery register	Capital expenditure budgets and discounted cash flow statements for the assessment of project profitability
6. Annual profit and loss account and balance sheet	Periodic (short-term) profit and loss accounts, balance sheets and operating reports

NATURE OF BUDGETARY CONTROL SYSTEMS

3. Relationship of budgetary control to business functions. Budgetary control is both a planning and a control technique, embracing all business functions. An essential requirement for the effective use of this technique is the involvement of all functional managers and supervisors responsible for the operation of functions, departments, or sections.

The managers are responsible for actively participating in the preparation of budgets outlining their operational responsibilities, on the premise that they cannot be held accountable for the achievement of objectives they have not participated in establishing. The setting of budgets in this way involves an important management activity, that of planning.

The control element of budgetary control is accomplished by comparing the actual results achieved with the planned results and noting significant variances necessitating corrective action by appropriate managers and supervisors (*see* Table XI).

4. Definition of a budget. "A financial and/or quantitative statement, prepared and approved prior to a defined period of time, of the policy to be pursued during that period for the purpose of attaining a given objective. It may include income, expenditure and the employment of capital."

Although a budget is prepared prior to a defined period of time and is similar to a forecast, which is an assessment of probable future events, it is not in itself a forecast. A budget is based on the implications of a forecast, which must precede the preparation of a budget, and relates to a planned course of action after the facts disclosed in a forecast have been considered. Figure 17 outlines the budget structure of a typical manufacturing business.

5. Budget period. Although the normal budget period is one year, to coincide with the financial year, it is necessary to analyse the annual budget into monthly short-term budgets, often referred to as monthly operating or control periods. This is essential so that the information disclosed in short-term operating statements may provide the basis for remedial action during the subsequent operating period, thereby avoiding the shortcomings of annual historical accounting reports. The results of operations may also be reported on a daily or weekly basis, depending upon the importance of the factors involved.

6. Principal Budget Factor. The factor on which the foundation of a budget is based is referred to as the Principal Budget Factor and it must be identified before the preparation of budgets commences. For example, the available production capacity may be capable of producing higher outputs than the anticipated sales

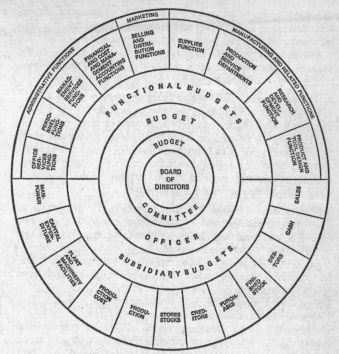

FIG. 17   *Budget structure.*

potential. In this instance, the potential sales is the Principal Budget Factor on which the budget must be based, as it is not feasible to produce items for which there is no sales potential unless there are other reasons for doing so—to maintain full employment for instance.

On the other hand, it may be found that potential sales exceed the output capabilities of the existing production capacity. The problem may be overcome by sub-contracting operations normally carried out in the factory which, in effect, increases the available capacity of both machines and manpower.

When production capacity exceeds potential sales, a positive approach requires to be made to generate additional sales, perhaps by advertising campaigns.

7. Budget centre. A budget centre may be defined as a section of the organisation of an undertaking, for the purposes of budgetary control. A section of an undertaking may be a function, department, section, machine or person. Functional budgets are prepared for each of the functions of the business, indicating the income and expenditure appropriate to a specific function for a defined period of time.

8. Presentation of budget drafts. Initial budget drafts are submitted to a budget committee for consideration. It is very unusual for such drafts to be accepted on their first presentation, owing to a number of reasons such as insufficient profit, inadequate profit when related to sales, or inadequate turnover of assets in relation to sales, etc. When appropriate adjustments have been effected, the budget drafts are re-presented to the budget committee until, eventually, they are provisionally approved.

9. Presentation of budgets to board of directors. The budget plans, after provisional approval by the budget committee, are then placed before the board of directors for their approval. If unacceptable, the reasons are indicated and appropriate redrafting is effected in accordance with the requirements of the board. Unfortunately, if the sales budget, for instance, is unacceptable, then redrafting has repercussions throughout the related production budget, production cost budget, purchasing budget, stock budgets, manpower budgets and other functional budgets.

After adjustments have been effected and resubmitted and, it is hoped, finally approved, the budgets indicate the course of action to be pursued during the forthcoming budget period to achieve objectives.

10. Advantages of budgetary control. When used effectively, budgetary control systems can provide a wide range of advantages to a business, because the system provides a means of navigation which assists a business in arriving at its destination without unnecessary deviation from its required course. The business is able to detect variations off course and apply corrective trim immediately, as it is able to check where it should be at short-time intervals. Without such a system, a business is likely to wander off course and not realise the situation until the required destination is out of reach. It may then be too late to retrace its course, as the point of no return may have been reached and resources are insufficient to do so. One might say the engines would run out of fuel. This metaphorical outline means, of course, that it is essential for a business to have a plan to guide it in its operations, to achieve a defined set of goals or objectives. By comparing results with the plan, frequently it is able to detect variances, often adverse, which will prevent the achievement of objectives, unless corrective action is taken immediately.

The most important objectives of budgetary control are summarised below:

(a) Defines the objectives of the business as a whole.

(b) Defines the objectives of each budget centre.

(c) Reveals the extent to which actual results have achieved, or failed to achieve, the objectives for each budget centre for the purpose of applying remedial action.

(d) Facilitates the planning and control of income and expenditure, to secure the highest possible profit so as to ensure an adequate return on the assets employed in business operations.

(e) Provides the means of establishing standard costs with regard to budgeted overheads to be absorbed by products.

(f) Provides a basis for assessing performance of managers responsible for budget centres.

(g) Ensures that all resources are effectively employed.

(h) Provides the means of establishing future policy or the revision of current policy.

(i) Provides a framework for implementing incentive schemes based on results achieved.

(j) Enables capital expenditure projects to be planned and controlled.

(k) Enables research and development projects to be planned and controlled.

(l) The financing of business operations is facilitated by means of cash budgets and cash flow statements.

(m) Provides the means for centralised control of all business operations.

(n) Facilitates the preparation of periodic budget control statements, profit and loss accounts and balance sheets.

NATURE OF STANDARD COSTING SYSTEMS

11. Standard costing. Standard costing is a means of controlling the cost of products by the comparison of actual costs with standard costs and the analysis of variances to their causes for remedial action. Standard costs are predetermined costs for materials, labour and overheads in respect of standard products and are compiled from data indicated in Table VII.

TABLE VII. SOURCE OF DATA FOR THE COMPILATION OF
STANDARD PRODUCT COSTS

Standard element	Source of data
1. Direct material:	
(a) Material specification	Product designer
(b) Material weights and standard sizes	Materials standards controller
(c) Saleable scrap and off-cuts	Materials standards controller
(d) Prices of materials and parts	Purchasing officer in collaboration with Management accountant
2. Direct labour:	
(a) Machine and other operations	Process engineer
(b) Operation times	Work study department by means of work measurement
(c) Grade of labour	Factory management in collaboration with Work study department
(d) Rates of pay	Personnel department
3. Factory overheads:	Management accountant's department calculates production department overhead absorption rates from budgets
(a) Production departments	
(b) Service departments	
4. Administration overheads	Management accountant's department calculates a rate of overhead absorption on the most suitable basis from budgets
5. Selling and distribution overheads	Management accountant's department calculates a rate of overhead absorption on the most suitable basis from budgets

12. Relationship of budgetary control and standard costing. Whereas budgetary control is a means of controlling the operations of the business as a whole, standard costing is a means of controlling the cost of products. Budgets incorporate standard product data and the compilation of standard product costs requires the inclusion of budgeted overheads. Even without formal budgetary control, it is necessary to prepare expenditure budgets for such purposes, even though such budgets may not be used for control purposes.

It is possible to control business operations by the technique of budgetary control alone, by establishing budgets for each budget centre, together with other subsidiary budgets, for comparison with the actual results achieved and reporting variances which require management attention. Some types of business do not, of course, manufacture standard products and cannot therefore apply the technique of standard costing. In other instances, businesses operate fully integrated budgetary control, standard costing and financial accounting systems.

13. Relationship of the production system and budgetary control and standard costing systems. Wages documents from production budget centres are analysed to establish totals for direct and indirect wages (*see* Fig. 18). In respect of direct wages, they are recorded in a Work-In-Progress account which records the wages incurred on production operations (*see* Fig. 19). If historical job costing is used, then the wages are recorded on cost sheets of the relevant jobs. If standard costing is in operation then the actual costs are compared with standard costs for the establishment of variances in respect of labour efficiency and wages rate (*see* Figs. 19 and 21). Indirect wages are recorded on the expenditure summary sheet of the appropriate budget centres, analysed by expense code (*see* Fig. 20).

The cost of other physical resources, such as materials and overheads, are input to the production system represented by the Work-In-Progress account (*see* Fig. 19). The outputs from the production system—completed products and partly finished products—are valued at standard factory cost. The standard cost of completed products is transferred to the Finished stock account (*see* Fig. 19).

Cost variances are calculated to disclose the difference between the actual cost of inputs and the standard values and budgeted costs of outputs. The variances are recorded on the opera-

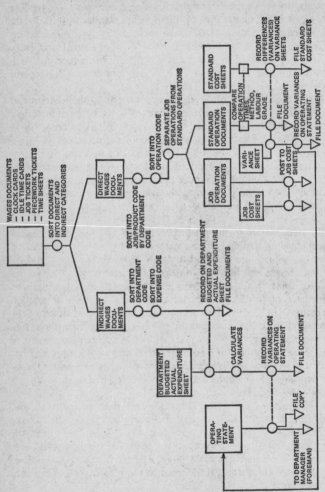

FIG. 18 *Wages analysis.*

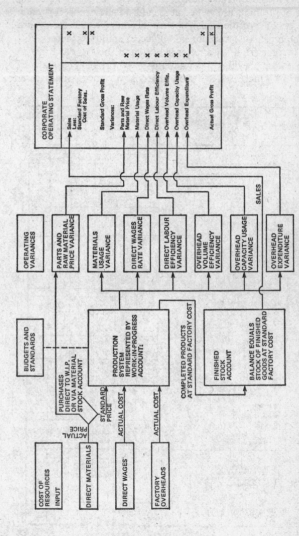

FIG. 19 *Relationship of production system and budgetary control and standard costing systems.*

ting statements of each budget centre (see Figs. 19 and 21).

Sales of products are valued at standard factory cost for reducing the balance of the Finished stock account, which then represents the finished stocks unsold valued at standard factory cost.

The income from sales, after subtracting the standard factory cost of sales, provides the standard gross profit. The standard gross profit is increased by favourable cost variances, and reduced

		Budget Centre: Press Shop					
Month: January 19..							
		Current Month			Year to Date		
Expense Code	Description	Budget	Actual	Variance	Budget	Actual	Variance
		(£)	(£)	(£)	(£)	(£)	(£)
	OPERATING LABOUR: WAGES						
	Assistant Foreman	143	150	7 (A)			
	Setters	115	125	10 (A)			
	Labourers	77	85	8 (A)			
	Shop Clerks	91	100	9 (A)			
	Sub-total	426	460	34 (A)			
	GENERAL OPERATING OVERHEADS:						
	Scrap	6	60	54 (A)			
	Rectification	6	50	44 (A)			
	Overtime Premium	3	10	7 (A)			
	Shift Premium	-	-				
	Holiday Pay	184	190	6 (A)			
	Make-up Allowance	6	5	1 (F)			
	National Insurance	67	70	3 (A)			
	Electricity (metered)	46	60	14 (A)			
	Waiting Time	6	40	34 (A)			
	Sub-total	324	485	16 (A)			
	CONSUMABLE SUPPLIES:						
	Small Tools	12	90	78 (A)			
	Lubricants	12	20	8 (A)			
	Consumable Materials	46	70	24 (A)			
	Works Stationery	6	10	4 (A)			
	Sub-total	76	190	114 (A)			
	TOTAL OVERHEADS CONTROLLABLE BY FOREMAN	826	1,135	309 (A)			
	EQUIPMENT COSTS:						
	Depreciation of Machines and Equipment	135	135	-			
	Maintenance Contracts	-	-	-			
	Spare Parts	23	115	92 (A)			
	Leasing Charges	-	-	-			
	Sub-total	158	250	92 (A)			
	TOTAL DEPARTMENTAL OVERHEADS-DIRECT	984	1,385	401 (A)			
	SERVICE DEPARTMENTS AND GENERAL FACTORY OVERHEAD ALLOCATION AND APPORTIONMENT	1,994	2,100	106 (A)			
	TOTAL DEPARTMENTAL OVERHEAD	2,978	3,485	407 (A)			

FIG. 20   *Budget and actual expenditure summary sheet.*

Month: January 19..		BUDGET CENTRE: Press shop	
	OPERATING RATIOS	Current Month	Year to date
		%	%
1.	Efficiency ratio	109	
2.	Use of capacity ratio	92	
3.	Activity ratio 1 x 2	100	
	COST VARIANCES		
	DIRECT LABOUR VARIANCES:	£	£
4.	Efficiency	250 (F)	
5.	Wage rate	275 (A)	
6.	Total 4-5	25 (A)	
	OVERHEAD VARIANCES:		
7.	Volume efficiency	250 (F)	
8.	Capacity usage	240 (A)	
9.	Volume 7-8	10 (F)	
10.	Expenditure	510 (A)	
11.	Total 9-10	500 (A)	

FIG. 21   *Budget centre operating statement.*

by adverse cost variances, which produces the actual gross profit (*see* Fig. 19).

The gross profit is reduced by subtracting the overheads incurred by the administrative and marketing functions, which produces the net profit of the business for the appropriate operating period.

14. Advantages of standard costing. The most important advantages attributed to the technique are summarised as follows.

(*a*) The comparison of actual with standard product costs provides the basis for assessing the efficiency of operations.

(*b*) Provides a means of selecting the most suitable materials and methods of manufacture.

(*c*) Provides a basis for calculating variances for "management by exception" reporting techniques.

(*d*) Minimises the recording of cost data as only changes to standard data need be recorded.

(*e*) The valuation of stocks is facilitated by means of standard cost rates.

(*f*) Facilitates the preparation of budgets by the use of standard product data.

(*g*) Provides the basis for the revision of selling prices in accordance with standard cost revisions.

(*h*) Facilitates the calculation of operating ratios with which to assess the efficiency of performance.

PROGRESS TEST 5

1. Specify the functions of management accounting systems, indicating the relationships which exist between financial and management accounting systems.   (1, 2 and Table VI)

2. Indicate the nature of budgetary control systems and compile a list of advantages attributable to such systems.   (3–10)

3. Indicate the nature of standard costing systems and compile a list of advantages attributable to such systems.   (11–14 and Table VII)

CHAPTER VI

Conceptual Aspects of Business Systems

Having established the nature of non-financial and financial systems in III and IV, it is now appropriate to examine a number of conceptual factors appertaining to business systems, regarding systems relationships and integration.

SYSTEMS RELATIONSHIPS

1. Input/output relationships. In many cases systems have a direct relationship because, in many instances, the output from one is the input to another, even though they may be administered as separate systems. This may be due to the way in which the systems first came into existence, but in many instances the input/output relationship has been the basis for integrating such systems to take advantage of administrative efficiency, which larger systems often achieve.

An example of a system, whereby the output from one system provides the input to another, is in respect of production planning and control (*see* Fig. 10). Works order documentation consisting of operation job cards, progress tickets, material requisitions, route card and inspection tickets is issued to manufacturing departments, in respect of each works order, by the production planning and control department. When manufacturing departments complete each operation, the relevant progress ticket is returned to production control for updating production schedules for control purposes (*see* Fig. 11). In effect, the progress ticket is a "turnround" document because, initially, it was an output from the production control system and an input to the production system.

The initial output document then becomes an input document for further processing. Copies of the progress tickets, in the form of operation job cards (sometimes called job tickets or piecework tickets), are sent to the wages office—which is an output from the production system and an input to the wages system—for calculating each operator's gross wages, preparation of the payroll, pay-

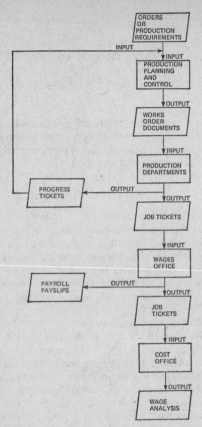

FIG. 22   *System input/output relationships.*

slips and tax and earnings records. The operation job cards are then passed to the cost office for the analysis of wages for purposes of cost control (*see* Fig. 22). This is a further instance of output from one system providing the input to another, although the wages system did not produce the operation job cards in the first instance (*see* 5).

2. Control relationships (control interface). Despatching source documents to the control system, the production system to the production planning and control system in the case indicated above, is a means of communication between the two types of sub-systems and forms what may be referred to as the "control interface". A further element of the control interface is the communication of plans by the planning and control system to the manager of the system subjected to control, i.e. the production system. In general, the control interface is the point at which physical sub-systems and related control sub-systems intersect, which may be termed the communications framework existing between the sub-systems.

The collection of information in respect of the output from a physical system, such as the production system, is the keystone of control and is, in fact, the "threshold" of the control system. The information is collected by means of a "sensor" which, in the case of the production system, would be a progress clerk for the *quantity* produced and an inspector for the *quality* of production. Such information is recorded on source documents. It is possible to employ a sensor for counting or measuring purposes, in the form of a mechanical or electronic counter (*see* XI, **18–23**).

SYSTEMS INTEGRATION—THE SYSTEMS APPROACH

3. Systems integration defined. Systems integration is the combining of a number of related sub-systems to form a larger sub-system, or total system, embracing the whole of a business's operations, for the purpose of improving administrative efficiency. This is largely achieved by entering data into the system once only, thereby avoiding duplication of data recording and clerical (processing) operations and the elimination of copying errors. Systems integration is often facilitated by the output from one system providing the input to another (*see* **1**). Very often, an integrated system is facilitated by a central file containing information which is relevant to, and accessible by, the various functions concerned with the integrated system, thus eliminating duplicated files. In a large, computer-based integrated system this takes the form of a "databank" (*see* VII).

When integrated systems are being developed, it is advisable for representatives of the various functions concerned to be members of the investigation team. This enables their knowledge and experience to be applied to the design of the system which will then be more effective than it would be otherwise (*see* XI, **4**).

4. The systems approach to systems integration. Referring to I, **2**, it was stated that most systems are of a functional nature, serving the needs of specific functions. Some systems, however, are developed on the basis of a "total systems" philosophy embracing a number of functional systems. All business systems are related to each other to a greater, or lesser, extent. This must be so, because the business as a whole is a complete system comprising all of the functional systems.

When a business first comes into existence it is often a one-man concern and most of the information relating to business trans- actions is stored mentally by the proprietor. The proprietor may of course supplement his memory by the maintenance of simple records of items ordered and sold, how much he owes and how much he is owed, etc.

Problems arise when a business expands as this requires the structuring of separate functions, which the proprietor may delegate to a person(s) he has engaged for the purpose. This is necessary, since it is not possible for the proprietor to effect direct control over all the functional activities as he did before. In such cases, functional systems develop individually, as circumstances dictate, often in isolation from other functional systems, and this is the point when the objectives of the various functions tend to conflict with each other. As a result, although the functional systems are optimised, i.e. developed to achieve a defined purpose and objective, the business activities as a whole will be under-optimised, due to individual functional systems being out of balance with regard to business objectives as a whole. Various functional systems may require information of a common nature, which is often stored in separately structured files and, apart from the duplication of files, the danger is that the files of some functions may be updated regularly, and others less regularly, causing conflict when the information from the various sources is compared, either for control or decision-making purposes.

The foregoing may be referred to as the "piecemeal" approach to the development of business systems, which is not so efficient as the overall approach which is generally referred to as the "systems approach".

The "systems approach" to systems development recognises the relationships and inter-dependence of systems, particularly as the flow of information throughout the business transcends arbitrary, functional demarcation lines. This approach enables related sub-systems to be integrated to form a larger system.

Fundamental changes may be required for administering integrated systems, as they become inter-functional systems, rather than loosely connected functional systems. This factor must be recognised, since a greater degree of co-ordination and co-operation between managers is essential to ensure smooth operation, free of inter-functional conflict. It must not be overlooked, however, that the co-ordination of functional activities is one of the prime responsibilities of a managing director or general manager. All that is, perhaps, required is a greater appreciation of the purpose and objectives of the relevant systems.

There will be occasions when the functional organisation of a business may require restructuring, with the advent of systems integration, especially as the present tendency is for routine business data-processing requirements to be processed by computer (*see* 7). This is not to say that a computer is imperative to systems integration, but it is often considered the best processing method to use, to facilitate the response-time needs of systems with regard to information and its ability to process large volumes of data speedily and accurately.

5. Example of inter-functional, integrated sales accounting system. The purpose of the system is to prepare works order documents for customers' special order requirements, despatch documents for shipping goods to customers and invoices for despatch to customers, ledger posting and sales analysis. The principles involved in the system include the requirement that orders are to be edited by the sales department before acceptance, to ensure that all details are correct regarding quantity and specification. With standard products it would be necessary to check that product codes and/or catalogue numbers were correct and in accordance with the current range. The credit status of the customer must be checked and proved satisfactory before acceptance of the order, as it is one thing to make a sale, but it is another to obtain payment. It is important to check the delivery situation and to inform the customer of the anticipated delivery date. Figure 23 outlines the various functions and activities, the detail of which is summarised below.

(*a*) *Sales function.* Orders are received through the post (quotation stage omitted) and, after editing and checking credit and delivery status, are transferred to an internal order two-part set. One copy of the order is routed to the production planning and

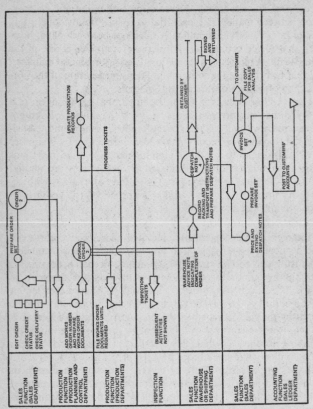

FIG. 23 *Inter-functional integrated sales accounting system.*

control department (production function), the other is filed for reference.

(b) *Production function.*

(i) *Production planning and control department.* A copy of the internal order is received from the sales function and from this is prepared a two-part works order document set. From this set, appropriate documents are routed through to the appropriate production and inspection departments. Orders are progressed by means of progress tickets, returned from the production departments. Upon completion of the order the warehouse is advised, so that they may prepare despatch notes, including packing and transport instructions. One works order set is retained on file for reference.

(ii) *Production and inspection departments.* In accordance with the instructions contained in the works order documentation the customer's order is manufactured. As stated above, when parts of the order are completed, progress tickets are returned to the production planning and control department, for updating production records for control purposes. Inspection departments are concerned with checking the *quality* of production, which need not concern the reader in this instance.

(c) *Warehouse or shipping department (part of sales function).* From the advice note advising of goods ready for despatch from the production planning and control department, a four-part despatch note set is prepared (after entering packing and transport instructions). Two copies of the despatch notes are sent with the goods, one copy is retained by the customer, the second copy is signed and returned by the customer, as proof of receipt of the goods. One copy of the despatch note is filed and the other sent to the sales department.

(d) *Sales function.* The copy of the despatch note received from the warehouse is priced and extended and a three-part invoice set is prepared from it. One copy is sent to the customer to inform him of his indebtedness for the goods supplied; one copy is sent to the sales ledger section of the accounting function, for recording on the customer's account, and then filed. The remaining copy is used for sales analysis.

6. Problems of implementing the "systems approach". A completely integrated business system is, in most instances, more of an ideal rather than a practical reality, which is something of a dilemma, considering the attributes which a "systems approach"

is said to have. Why is this? The answer to the question requires
a little deductive thinking which may be formulated as follows:

The "systems approach" involves complexity, necessitating a
detailed knowledge of systems relationships and the interdependence by the systems designers and administrative management.
Apart from the factors already outlined in this chapter, it is also
necessary to establish the information requirements of functions
and the information flows between functions. Accordingly a very
detailed analysis is required of relationships between inputs, files
and outputs, as well as types of information and the frequency
with which it is required by specific managers, for control and
decision making purposes. This means that the business must be
looked upon as a complex communications network. The very
task of collecting facts and defining their relationships is formidable in itself, but the design of integrated systems, providing for
all functional needs, is even more formidable.

Systems can only operate effectively if they are fully understood
by administrative management and their staff and integration can
detract from this, due to the added complexity of such systems. Of
course, Rome was not built in a day and this fact implies that
systems integration should be developed over a period of time, on
an evolutionary basis rather than a revolutionary basis.

A further important factor is the need to integrate systems, in
such a way that they operate smoothly and achieve the desired
objectives as effectively as possible. This also implies their development on a modular basis, for full integration at a later date
(*see* 10).

It has already been intimated that a computer may be the only
way to obtain the benefits of integration, to facilitate the response-
time needs of systems and the ability to process large volumes of
data speedily and accurately (*see* 4). A small computer may not
have sufficient storage capacity for processing integrated systems
applications, but this depends upon the design of computer runs,
the type of operating system required and whether integrated files,
in the form of a database, are used. This implies that it may only
be the larger type of business which can afford a high degree of
systems integration, due to the cost of the computer configuration
required for the purpose. Looking at this point in another way,
it may also mean that it is only the larger firm which needs a high
degree of integration for reasons of efficiency, because size often
generates systems-complexity, due to the many inter-relationships
which exist between functions and systems. Large firms tend to be

structured in a very detailed functional manner, with a high degree of specialisation, and it is this factor which may cause problems of integration. Once integration has been developed, however, the benefits to be gained may be enormous.

A smaller business may not require a high degree of integration of its systems, due to less complexity in its operations but, on the other hand, the systems may be much more simply combined than is possible for the larger business.

SYSTEMS INTEGRATION AND THE ROLE OF A COMPUTER

7. The systems approach and the computer. A total systems approach is likely to require the use of a computer, due to the highly complex inter-relationships of data-flows that need to be processed, in a suitable time-scale, for "system response-time" requirements. In addition, information needs to be stored in such a way that it may be retrieved by management on demand, by direct-access facilities. This may necessitate on-line or real-time processing using terminals (*see* IX, **15, 19**). It is in this type of situation that the speed and logical ability of a computer becomes imperative.

8. Integrated order-entry system. Many integrated systems are processed by computer, applying the batch-processing technique using a suite of programs which serve the needs of several functions. A notable example is an integrated order-entry system which is illustrated in Fig. 24. The run chart has a suite of programs as follows:

(*a*) Run 1. Order details on punched cards are validated and a printed report is produced indicating invalid items which are referred back to the sales office for correction. Valid items are recorded on magnetic tape. Control totals are also calculated and printed on the report.

(*b*) Run 2. Valid transactions are sorted into stock number sequence.

(*c*) Run 3. Stock records are input, in accordance with the items ordered, for the purpose of checking stock availability, pricing and calculating the value of items ordered. The stock file is stored on magnetic disc for direct access requirements. Satisfied order details and unsatisfied order details are recorded on separate magnetic tapes. A printed report is produced indicating those

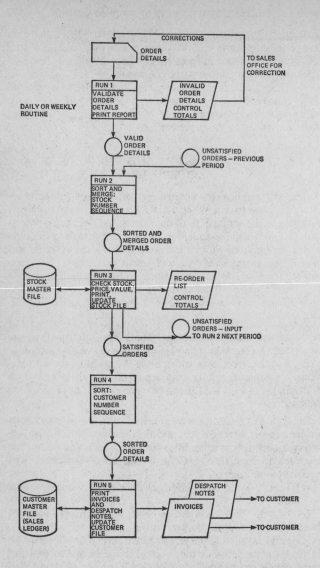

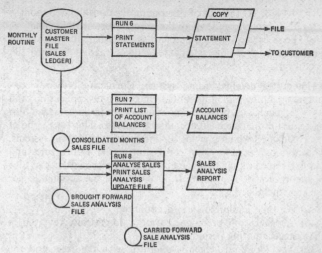

FIG. 24   *Integrated order entry system.*

items of stock which require replenishment. Control totals are also printed out. The unsatisfied orders tape will be input to Run 2 the next period. This will be consolidated with the current orders produced on magnetic tape by Run 1. The stock file is also updated for recording the current status of all stock items.

(*d*) Run 4. The satisfied orders, already priced and valued, are sorted to customer number sequence on magnetic tape.

(*e*) Run 5. Customer records stored on magnetic disc are input for printing customer's name and address details on invoices. Each customer's order details are input from the sorted tape produced in Run 4. From this tape item details in respect of product number, description, price, value and VAT are printed on invoices. Discount rates are then applied and the invoice for each customer is totalled, after all item details have been printed. The customer file (sales ledger file) is then updated with the value of goods supplied for recording the current balance owing by the customer. Despatch notes are also printed.

(*f*) Run 6 and 7. At the end of the month customer records are input and statements of account are printed for despatch to the customer. A list of account balances is also printed which may show an "age analysis" of the account balances.

(*g*) Run 8. At the end of the month, the consolidated months sales file is input together with the brought forward sales analysis file. The sales are analysed and a sales analysis report is printed. The sales analysis file is updated and a carried forward file produced.

9. Integrated nominal ledger system. Northern Software Consultants Limited, manufacturers of computer-application and software packages, provide a nominal ledger package which also incorporates management accounting features. This is just one of their packages which provide for integrated accounting systems. The nominal ledger system can be integrated with a sales and purchase accounting package and a fixed asset register can also be incorporated, etc. Some of the features of the nominal ledger package include:

(*a*) Automatic double entry accounting.

(*b*) Accruals and prepayments are automatically reversed in the next accounting period.

(*c*) The Nominal ledger is regarded as a database and the analysis printing program can report in any sort sequence and in many different formats any data held on the Nominal ledger.

(*d*) When linked with the Purchase ledger, standard monthly postings can be made automatically, such as Hire Purchase, insurance, rates, rent, etc.

(*e*) A History File of all transaction records can be maintained so that analysis and schedules can be produced at the year end.

(*f*) Profit and Loss statements, Balance Sheet and Operating Statements for management can be produced.

(*g*) Budgetary control can be exercised, producing variances from Budget.

(*h*) Budget flexing enables budgets to be altered by percentage changes, and produce financial projections as a result of the change.

(*i*) Nominal accounts can be re-analysed into Cost or Profit Centres, producing reports in up to seven different sort keys.

(*j*) A year end report produces a summary of each Nominal Account for each accounting period, compared to budget and/or previous year.

Figure 25 illustrates the computer runs for a nominal ledger system which is based on the system outline shown in Fig. 12. The input to Run 1 is derived from data produced by the separate computer applications, in respect of transactions relating to

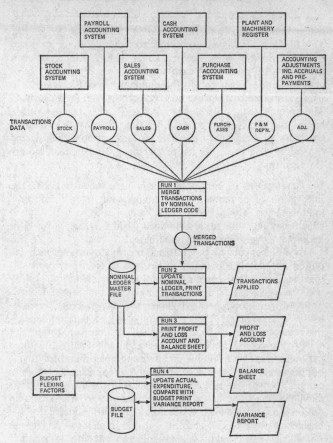

FIG. 25 *Run chart: computerised integrated nominal ledger system.*

stocks, payroll, sales, purchases, plant and machinery including depreciation, accruals and pre-payments, accounting adjustments and cash. The transaction data in respect of each application is assumed to be stored on magnetic tape. Run 1 is concerned with consolidating all nominal ledger data and this is achieved by merging all the relevant transactions on nominal ledger codes.

The output from Run 1 is a consolidated file of transactions, which is input to Run 2 for updating the nominal ledger file. This file is stored on magnetic disc to facilitate direct access to relevant nominal ledger account codes. Run 2 also produces a list of detailed postings to each account.

At the end of the month, the nominal ledger file is input to Run 3, to produce a Profit and Loss account and Balance sheet. The nominal ledger file is also input to Run 4, together with a budget file which is updated with actual expenditure providing the cumulative expenditure to date for comparison with budgeted expenditure. A variances report is then printed, analysed by Cost centre.

10. Development of integrated systems on a modular basis. The integration of computerised systems should be planned on a modular basis. This approach enables programs to be developed which may be more easily combined when a system is ready to be implemented, on an integrated basis.

For full benefits to be attained, the modular approach requires very detailed planning of projects to ensure systems slot together in an effective manner. Major reprogramming may otherwise be necessary. Current systems must be viewed from a futuristic standpoint, because plans made now generate improvements in the future. This is the only way of maintaining administrative efficiency, because sophisticated integrated computer systems cannot be implemented overnight. The many integrated package programs available facilitate the upgrading of systems, but they need to be appraised very carefully to ensure that they are compatible with the system requirements of the business. This is facilitated, to some extent, because package programs contain optional modules, which enable the ones most suitable for the business to be selected, checked out and implemented. The use of packages can speed up systems enhancement since they reduce the internal (user) programming effort. Care needs to be taken, however, that systems are not "bent" to suit the characteristics of packages, unless by doing so additional benefits are obtained to those provided by the current systems. The use of standard package programs eliminates to some extent the duplication of effort in developing systems in different organisations which are basically similar.

SYSTEMS INTEGRATION AND THE CHANGING ROLE OF MIDDLE MANAGEMENT

11. New responsibilities. With the development of computerised integrated systems, the role of middle management, i.e. departmental managers, is likely to change. Probably the main reason for this is the transfer of data-processing activities, for which middle managers were formerly responsible, to the computer. Due to this factor, the number of staff in specific departments concerned with invoicing, payroll, stock control and general accounting activities, may be reduced. Consequently, there may be a need to restructure departments requiring managers to take on new responsibilities.

Also, due to the greater complexity of integrated systems, managers will be required to participate to a greater extent in the development of such systems. This may require a greater degree of capability from managers, even though they may control a smaller number of staff. They will, for instance, need to exercise strict control over the timeliness and accuracy of data being presented to the computer department for processing.

12. Reports and routine decision making. Middle managers, in many cases, will relinquish the role of data processors, which they were formerly required to be when they were responsible for compiling reports for their superiors—the functional managers—as this role is often taken over by a computer.

Routine decision making, often the role of middle managers, is often computerised as computer programs are developed for making structured decisions. This type of decision is so called, because it conforms to a standard set of rules; a typical example being the automatic ordering of stock by an exception report, when individual items of stock fall to a predefined re-order level.

SYSTEMS INTEGRATION AND THE CENTRALISATION OF DECISION MAKING

13. Centralisation of computing. It was stated previously (*see* 7) that it is often necessary to computerise integrated systems and this may lead to the centralisation of decision making. This may arise when the major business systems of a group of companies are facilitated by centralised computing services. Such an arrangement will require remote job-entry facilities, whereby data for processing is transmitted to the computer from each of the operating units and the results transmitted back (*see* IX, **21**). In addition, on-line information retrieval facilities will need to be provided, by means of terminals, to enable managers to gain access to information files as the need arises (*see* Appendix IV and IX, **19**).

The advantages of this arrangement are obtained by being able to process the data of all operating units more speedily and the provision of management information on demand, for decision making and control. Managers are then able to take action in a more appropriate time-scale, while the situation is current, rather than historical. One of the principal features of a centralised service is that incoming data, when processed, can be compared with budgets, standards or targets of performance, the appropriate parameters being stored in the computer's files, and the "exceptions", in the form of variances, reported to managers of decentralised operating units. But what of centralised decision making? It was first necessary to indicate the basic features of a centralised computing service before embarking on the study of centralised decision making. The reader is now directed to **14** where this aspect is outlined.

14. Centralised decision making. In addition to, or instead of, remote job entry facilities, centralised decision making may necessitate on-line updating of application files, to ensure that up-to-date information is available for retrieval purposes. If it is considered that the several companies in the group are controlled by a main board of directors at head office, then the board will have information available with which to monitor the operations of the group.

Monitoring is for the purpose of ensuring that achievements accord with the corporate objectives, which may be modified if current circumstances indicate the necessity of doing so. Decentralised managers of operating units in the group may then be informed of such changes for implementation.

It is possible that tactical decisions may also be made centrally, in addition to strategic decisions, but it is more likely that this class of decision will be made by decentralised management, working within the guidelines of corporate policy. If all classes of decision were made centrally, then this would stifle the initiative of decentralised management. It would also result in decisions being made too remote from the scene of operations, which is not good practice, because basic information may not disclose the full facts of a situation. Some decisions have to be made on facts of an unquantifiable nature: those, for instance, which relate to management and personnel conflicts, relationships with customers and suppliers, etc.

Centralised decision making may result in some decisions being made at the incorrect management level, particularly routine operating decisions, which are best made in the dispersed operating units by local management. Otherwise top management would have less time to consider more important decisions of a strategic nature.

PROGRESS TEST 6

1. Input/output relationships are very often considered to be a suitable basis for the integration of systems to obtain administrative efficiency which larger systems often achieve. Indicate the input/output relationships in a production planning and control system. (1)

2. Many of the problems and difficulties of communication are inherent in information systems. Discuss how such problems and difficulties can be minimised. (2)

(I.A.M. W1974, Part A, Q7)

3. State your understanding of the following terms:

(*a*) control interface, and

(*b*) threshold of control system. (2)

4. What do you understand by the term "systems integration"? (3)

5. It is common in the development of integrated systems to establish multi-disciplinary teams drawn from various parts of an organisation. Discuss the rationale behind this approach and comment on its practical implications. (3 and XI, 4)

(I.A.M. W1974, Paper A, Q2)

6. For what ideals would a designer strive regarding source data in an integrated system? What difficulties are likely to preclude the achievement of such ideals? (3 and VII, 2)

(I.A.M. W1973, Paper No. 1, Q5)

7. What is the "total systems concept"? How valid is the concept and what difficulties are likely to be encountered when introducing it into an organisation? (4, 6)

(I.A.M. S1973, Paper No. 1, Q1)

8. What effect is functional organisation likely to have on the systems which support it?   (4)   (I.A.M. S1975, Paper A, Q4)

9. In what ways, and to what extent, will a systems approach enhance the efficiency of the administrative management of an organisation?   (4)   (I.A.M. W1973, Paper No. 1, Q7)

10. What is "the systems approach" and how does it assist the administrative management process?   (4)

(I.A.M. W1974, Part A, Q6)

11. It may be argued that since functional analysis is of value in the development of integrated data processing, it is logical to re-structure an organisation in this way, i.e. functionally. Discuss this viewpoint and comment on the effect of such a re-organisation on other organisational factors, e.g. control.   (4)

(I.A.M. W1973, Paper No. 1, Q4)

12. In an integrated system, the interdependence of the parts becomes important. Discuss this phenomenon and comment on its desirability.   (4)   (I.A.M. S1974, Part A, Q4)

13. Give an example of an inter-functional sales accounting system.   (5)

14. Since the analysis stage of a project is the foundation on which design can be built, it is a critical factor in eventual success. Discuss this point of view and propose methods of analysis aimed at achieving maximum effectiveness.   (6)

(I.A.M. W1974, Part B, Q8)

15. A number of writers have suggested that the development of management information systems is a mirage. In essence, they are suggesting that one integrated system, even allowing for the use of a computer, cannot meet the requirements of management. Discuss this apparent conflict with the total systems concept.   (4)

(I.A.M. W1973, Paper No. 2, Q4)

16. Why is the "total systems approach" likely to require the use of a computer?   (7)

17. Prepare a run chart of a computerised integrated order-entry system.   (8)

18. Prepare a computer run chart for an integrated nominal ledger system.   (9)

19. A short-cut to the development of computer-based systems is afforded by applications packages. Discuss the utility of packages and the desirability of their use.   (10) (I.A.M. S1974, Part A, Q5)

20. Many people have deplored the apparent duplication of effort in developing systems in different organisations. There is little doubt that great similarities exist between an organisation's

requirements and those of others, particularly in the same industry. Critically discuss this phenomenon and comment upon attempts to avoid such duplication. **(10)** (I.A.M. W1975, Paper II, Q8)

21. In an organisation which has adopted the systems concept, suggest how the concept would be manifested in planning procedures. Discuss also how the procedures may differ in other approaches. **(10)**   (I.A.M. S1975, Paper A, Q2)

22. How is the use of a computer for data processing likely to affect the clerical work of an organisation? **(11)**

(I.A.M. W1973, Paper I, Q8)

23. It could be argued that with the development of integrated information systems the role of middle management will change. Discuss the likelihood of this possibility, the reasons for its occurrence, and the possible form it will take. **(11, 12)**

(I.A.M. W1973, Paper 2, Q6)

24. Increasingly, in the development of systems, mathematical tools and techniques are becoming an integral part of those systems. Is this development likely to increase the automatic decision-making aspect of systems and to reduce the need for manual intervention? **(12)**   (I.A.M. S1974, Part A, Q2)

25. Fears have been expressed by many people that the development of integrated systems leads inevitably to the centralisation of decision making, thus reducing the influence of staff in other departments. Are such fears groundless and, if not, is this a desirable phenomenon? **(13, 14)**   (I.A.M. W1974, Part B, Q6)

CHAPTER VII

Database and Management Information Systems

CONCEPTUAL ASPECTS OF A DATABASE

1. What is a database? A database or databank may be defined as a collection of structured data supporting the operations of the whole, or major areas, of a business. It may also be defined as a centrally located data file providing the foundations of a computer-based management information system.

The concept of a database means something very specific and the collection of data must have certain qualities. The following definition was given by Floyd Johnson of Honeywell-Bull at an NCC conference on databases in 1973. "A non-redundant collection of all data serving one or more defined business applications, that data being structurally linked to and permitting access to all other data in that collection for which a natural or logical business relationship has been defined to exist, however complex."

An essential requirement of a database is not merely to store data efficiently, but also to provide an effective means of retrieval. The objective of a database is to provide reliable, up-to-date, unambiguous information on demand. The centralisation of information in itself serves no purpose but if it can be retrieved more efficiently than is otherwise possible then the data structure of a business may be rationalised.

The term "data" in the context of a database refers to a collection of data elements which, when related in a logical manner, provides meaningful information.

A database to be of any use at all must be maintained in an up-to-date condition. In a large-volume situation, such as the Driver and Vehicle Licensing Centre operations, this can present a formidable task in view of the number of transactions to be effected each day.

Similarly, file maintenance creates an additional work load for dealing with the deletion of obsolete, and the addition of new, records in respect of employees, customers and suppliers, etc.

2. Essential considerations for setting up a database. Traditionally, functions have developed their own files to support their specific operations. Such files are used for reference purposes, or are updated with transaction data, in order to provide the latest status of stocks, customer and supplier balances, etc. Such files often consist of records containing common data elements which are duplicated in several functional files. This situation creates redundancy, as the same data elements in each of the files are updated separately. The Personnel function, for instance, maintains a file of employee records, containing data elements in respect of an employee's name, address, number, marital status, department number, grade and rate of pay, etc. Similar data elements are also stored on the Payroll file, used in the preparation of wages and maintaining a record of earnings and tax. An input of current transaction data is required for each application, to update relevant data elements (*see* Fig. 26).

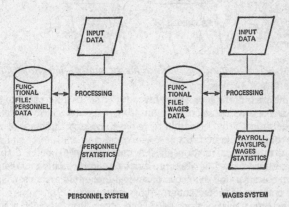

PERSONNEL SYSTEM   **WAGES SYSTEM**

FIG. 26 *Functional (sub-system) approach to file structures—multiple files.*

A database system aims at eliminating such duplication of storage and updating and providing the means for retrieving data elements for each of the application requirements, in the required combinations. All data relating to a specific subject (employees in this case), are then consolidated on an integrated file structure basis, rather than fragmented on a functional file basis (*see* Fig. 27).

When separate files are maintained with common data elements,

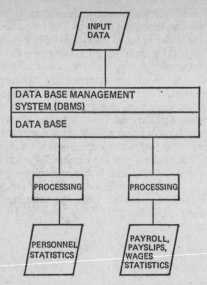

FIG. 27   *Database approach to file structures—integrated files.*

some are out of phase with others, due either to different updating cycles or frequencies, or even omitting to update a file completely.

The ideal situation would be to have one large database serving the needs of the business as a whole, but this leads to complexity in defining data relationships. A database need not be a single file, however, as it is often practicable to implement several small databases serving the needs of several integrated systems, that is, several sets of functional groupings, in respect of functions which have direct relationships with each other. For example, a Sales accounting system may be integrated to provide for invoicing and stock control. A Product file would provide data elements in respect of product code and description, cost price, selling price, VAT rate, stock balance, history of stock movements, etc. A Customer file would provide data elements in respect of customer code number, name, address for invoicing and address for delivery (if different from the invoice address), credit limit, account balance, account balance age analysis and sales history. The Product file would enable stock schedules and re-order lists to be printed out on demand. The Customer file would enable lists of account balances, accounts which had exceeded credit limit, age analysis of account balances, profitability reports and statements of account to be printed out as required.

One of the problems of setting up a database, for systems integration purposes, is the classification of data elements, as each must be allocated a data name for identification purposes. Data elements may be known by different names in the various functions and a data classification scheme is therefore essential before a database can be got off the ground. A data dictionary, consisting of data definitions, characteristics and inter-relationships, is therefore very necessary (*see* 12).

It is also necessary to specify data requirements for various functional needs, as indicated in the examples outlined previously, with regard to the personnel/payroll application and the integrated sales accounting system. The logical data relationships must also be defined. Only by this approach is it possible to design effective file-handling methods, which must take into account the operating needs for accessing data, rather than the manner in which data is stored physically.

Important factors related to the use of databases are summarised below:

(*a*) Data should be input only once.

(*b*) Redundant data should be eliminated.

(*c*) Data should be capable of being speedily retrieved.

(*d*) Files should be easy to maintain.

(*e*) Files should be expandable.

(*f*) Access to files should be capable of being restricted to authorised users by the use of passwords.

(*g*) Restart and recovery procedures are necessary.

(*h*) Selective print-outs should be provided for the requirements of specific managers.

(*i*) Provision should be made for batch and on-line processing.

(*j*) New data structures should be capable of being incorporated into the database.

(*k*) Distinction should be made between the physical and the logical storage of data.

(*l*) Should be capable of contending with changing circumstances within the business.

(*m*) Storage costs should be optimised.

(*n*) Should be self-monitoring including the provision of audit trails.

DATABASE MANAGEMENT SYSTEM (DBMS)

3. What is a database management system? It is a highly complex software package for creating, updating and extracting information from a computer-oriented database. There are a number of DBMS packages available, amongst which are those listed below.

(*a*) ADABAS—Adaptable Data Base Management System (Software A.G.).

(*b*) BDMS—Burroughs' Data Management System.

(*c*) DMS 1100—Univac Data Management System—1100 series.

(*d*) IDS—Integrated Data Store (Honeywell).

(*e*) IMS—Information Management System (IBM).

(*f*) RAMIS—Random Access Management Information System (Mathematica).

(*g*) System 2000—Product of Management Research International.

(*h*) TOTAL—Product of Cincom Systems.

4. Example of a DBMS package. As an example, the IDS package of Honeywell is a DBMS using Cobol as a host-language, which provides users with a simplified and easy-to-use method for record processing, using mass-storage, random-access devices. It is a general purpose system which can be used to build a variety of databases ranging from a simple file serving an individual application up to and including a complex integrated database serving an entire business.

The package contains the following elements:

(*a*) Data Description Language (DDL) (providing extensions to the Cobol Data Division).

(*b*) Data Manipulation Language (DML) (providing extensions to Cobol Procedure Division).

(*c*) A Translator which operates in conjunction with the Cobol compiler.

(*d*) Run-time software.

(*e*) Support utilities.

(*f*) User documentation.

The Data Description Language (DDL) allows records to be defined and fields within records to be named and the type of field specified, i.e. whether numeric, alphabetic or alphanumeric. In addition, the DDL is used to specify the required logical links so that a hierarchy or network of records can be established.

The Data Manipulation Language (DML) provides the processing instructions which allow programs operating under a DBMS to store, find and retrieve data records on the database. This adds to the processing capabilities of a Cobol procedure division.

Supporting utility programs assist in creating and loading the database, maintaining and auditing the database, etc.

LOGICAL DATA RELATIONSHIPS

5. Data elements. In the everyday use of our language, it is well known that characters make up words. Words in the context of data-processing may be classed as "fields", or data elements, such as a customer's account number, quantity ordered, price, and value, etc. A series of related data-elements constitute "records". From this, it can be seen that logical relationships exist between data-elements which may be very simple or complex. In setting up a database, it is essential to be aware of all such relationships. It is also important to appreciate logical relationships before making changes to particular data-elements, otherwise disruption will occur, as certain functions will not be able to access data-elements in the form they are required.

The Database Task Group (DBTG) initially recognised the three generally accepted definitions of structural data relationships as:

(a) Sequential List Structures.

(b) Tree Structures.

(c) Complex Network Structures.

It was also considered that the totality of data in a business may be a combination of all three.

6. Sequential list structure. A structure in which each element is related to the element preceding it and the element following it.

7. Tree structure. A hierarchical structure in which each element may be related to any number of elements at any level below it, but only one element above it in the hierarchy.

8. Network structure. Similar to a tree structure but with the important exception that any element may be related to any number of other elements. This type of structure closely represents the logical data relationships which exist in the world of business.

9. Sets. The DBTG concept of "sets" may be used to define the structures indicated above. The concept of sets is fundamental to understanding any file management technique related to "lists".

(*a*) A set is a collection of named record types.

(*b*) Any number of sets may be defined in a database.

(*c*) A set must have a single "owner" type, i.e. a master-record relating to a department for instance.

(*d*) A record type may be "owner" of one or more sets.

(*e*) A record type may be a "member" in one or more sets, e.g. details of employees may be a "member" of a personnel department set and a manufacturing department set.

(*f*) A record type may be both owner and member but in different sets.

(*g*) A set must have a specified set order.

10. Storage aspects. Direct access storage devices, such as discs, have made the use of databases possible, particularly by means of the technique of "virtual" storage. The technique increases the apparent capacity of internal storage, as programs are split into "pages", and only those which are required for processing are called into the internal memory. The remainder of the program remains on disc storage—virtual storage—until required.

Virtual storage is necessary in most database systems, because of the large storage capacity required for DBMS software, especially when it includes data communication facilities for on-line processing.

Discs also allow pointer techniques to be used, which are required when dealing with overflow conditions on the disc tracks, so that records can be located when they are out of sequence. This applies to index-sequential and random-file organisation. Discs may also have chained records either within a file or in other files. By this means it is possible to build up logical relationships between non-contiguous records.

DATABASE ADMINISTRATOR

11. The database administrator as a co-ordinator. As the whole concept of a database is to rationalise business systems by the integration of such systems, it follows that the data needs of an organisation must be co-ordinated at a very high level. This is basically the responsibility of a database administrator, who may not yet exist in many organisations. Nevertheless, someone has no doubt been vested with such responsibilities, perhaps a senior member of the systems staff.

When data is common to two or more applications, then programmers are not allowed the freedom they previously enjoyed to name data-elements and subject them to processing, independently of other application requirements. This is where the database administrator assumes command, as it were, because he must consider the data needs of the several applications under consideration, for consolidation into a database.

12. Duties of a database administrator. He must first of all be conversant with business policy and strategy, particularly for the long term, as the very fabric of a business is dependent upon an efficient and effective management information system, of which a database is a fundamental part—the roots of such a system in fact. He should play an active part in the planning of information systems, particularly with regard to feasibility studies.

He should be an expert in all file management techniques and be able to advise management and system planners of the capabilities and shortcomings of various file management systems, with regard to the application under review. It is essential that he liaise and consult with project teams on the development of design specifications, program specifications, systems documentation and programs, etc. It is imperative that he monitor the implementation of a database, ensuring that time and cost constraints are adhered to. Of extreme importance is the need for the administrator to ensure that system objectives are achieved. Also of importance is that the initial preparation and maintenance of a data dictionary should be the responsibility of a database administrator, as this is essential for the success of a database system (*see* 2).

PROGRESS TEST 7

1. What do you understand by the term database or databank? **(1)**

2. State what you consider to be essential considerations for implementing a database. **(2)**

3. What are the technical and commercial difficulties of developing a computer-based databank? **(1, 2)**

(I.A.M. S1973, Paper 2, Q6)

4. Discuss the nature of the databank and examine the reality of its underlying concepts. **(2)**   (I.A.M. S1975, Paper B, Q2)

5. The development of databanks has resulted in changes to the kind of information on file, the type of processing, and, in a wider sense, a changing role for the computer. Discuss fully the implications of these changes. **(1–12)** (I.A.M. W1975, Paper 11, Q5)

6. What is a database management system? **(3, 4)**

7. In setting up a database it is essential to be aware of data relationships. Give examples of structural data relationships that may exist in business systems. **(5–9)**

8. Direct access storage devices, such as magnetic discs, have made the use of databases possible particularly by means of the technique of "virtual" storage. Define "virtual" storage and state the purpose it serves. **(10)**

9. State why you consider a database administrator may be necessary outlining the duties you would expect the post to have. **(11, 12)**

CHAPTER VIII

Computers and Business Systems: Managerial, Organisational and Implementation Factors

WHAT IS A COMPUTER?

Although various aspects of computers were discussed in VI, within the context of a particular systems concept, it is considered that a formal introduction of computers at this point will be amply justified.

1. Computer configuration. A computer is not one machine, but a number of related machines, referred to as "hardware". The specific combination of machines used in a particular computer system is referred to as a "configuration". A computer configuration contains a central processing unit and input, storage and output devices known as "peripherals".

A computer may, therefore, be defined as a system which accepts data from an input device, performs operations on the data by means of the processor and transfers the results to an output device (*see* Fig. 28).

2. Basic features of a computer. A computer is "automatic" in operation, in the sense that, when the program and data for processing have been input to the processor's memory, the required output is produced without manual intervention, as all the program instructions are executed automatically.

Computers used for commercial data processing are "digital", as distinct from "analog", which are used for scientific and engineering applications. Digital computers process discrete numerical digits, representing business data in coded form (i.e. binary code), whereby a pulse of electricity represents 1 and no pulse represents 0. It is by such combinations of 1s and 0s that numerical, alphabetical and special characters are represented in the language of the computer.

An analog computer represents physical variables, such as rates

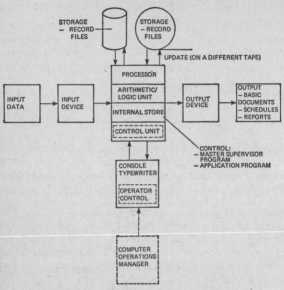

FIG. 28   *Electronic computer system.*

of flow, temperature or pressure by analogy, using variations of electrical voltage proportional to physical variables.

A computer consists of electronic circuits and components, through which pulses of electricity flow, representing data. Modern computers have integrated circuits, very small in size, allowing very high processing speeds to be achieved in the nanosecond range (one-thousandth of a microsecond—American billionth of a second). Hence the term "electronic" computer.

Computers have internally-stored programs, containing all the instructions necessary to process data to achieve particular results for a defined application, such as payroll, stock ledger or sales invoicing, etc. The "stored program" concept is very important, as it is this feature which enables a computer to cycle through the program to perform arithmetic and logic operations on data, as necessary, for a defined purpose. By this means, it is possible to 'loop" to a series of instructions repeatedly, so that each unit of data is processed in the same way. It is also the means whereby data may be compared and, according to its condition, cause the program to "branch" to a defined series of instructions to deal with the situation (*see* XI, **16, 17**).

3. Data preparation and data capture. Before processing can commence, data must first (in most cases) be converted into a "machine sensible" form. This is achieved by "data preparation" operations.

The traditional methods of data capture and preparation of data for processing utilise punched cards or paper tape and this involves a number of time-consuming and costly stages as shown below:

(*a*) Recording data on source documents in respect of internal transactions.

(*b*) Checking accuracy of data.

(*c*) Transferring data to a punching document to ensure high punching speeds, by marshalling source data elements from source documents into the field punching sequence on cards or paper tape. This procedure is often found to be beneficial with regard to external documents coming into the business. Such documents may be sales orders and purchase invoices which have a high degree of variability in their layout and data sequence. It takes considerable time to search for data-elements to be punched in the correct sequence, which slows down the punching operation appreciably.

(*d*) Punching data into cards or paper tape.

(*e*) Verifying data to ensure accuracy of punching.

(*f*) Correcting punching errors.

(*g*) Inputting data to computer.

(*h*) Validating and converting data to magnetic media, to obtain advantage of higher data transfer speed during subsequent runs.

New methods, however, do not necessarily follow a similar pattern, as they aim at shortening or accelerating the cycle of preparing data for processing. Paper tape, for instance, may be captured (punched) as a by-product of an accounting machine posting operation, whereby relevant data is punched into paper tape as posting takes place. The paper tape is then immediately available for input to a computer, which eliminates the need to punch and verify data as a separate operation.

Pre-punched tags are attached to items, such as garments in a retail store, and when the items are sold the tags are removed and sent to the computer in batches for processing. Although punching is not eliminated, it takes place before a transaction occurs, thereby reducing the time between an event occurring and processing the relevant data. By this means management information is available sooner, which facilitates the control of operations.

An Electricity Board produces consumer bills by computer in optical characters, detailing the account number and amount owing. An advice slip is detached from the bill by the consumer and presented with the money or cheque in payment. The advice slip is input to the computer to update the consumer's account. The method completely eliminates separate data preparation operations, as the computer has produced its own input at an earlier output stage. The advice slip is known as a "turnaround document".

In addition to the method of encoding data to magnetic tape by a keyboard encoder, a more sophisticated method enables an operator to visually check her work since data is displayed on a cathode ray tube (CRT), when data is keyed in from source documents. To enable keyboard errors to be reduced, magnetic tape cassettes are available, which have a special format for display on the CRT, which is a replica of the source document. The operator prepares computer input as if completing a form on a typewriter. As data is keyed in, it is displayed in the appropriate data boxes, which enables the operator to visually check and correct the data, when necessary, before depressing a "send" key which causes the data to be recorded on magnetic tape.

On-line data collection systems are also used for the speedy collection of data from dispersed locations (*see* IX, **22**).

Key-to-disc systems enable data to be accumulated on magnetic disc from a number of keyboards used by individual operators. A variation of this method is the ICL Key-Edit system, which collects data from up to sixteen keyboards on to a magnetic drum. The hub of the system is the Key-Edit processor, which controls record formatting, editing, input/output and file organisation on a real-time basis. As the majority of data-vetting operations are performed by the Key-Edit system, the computer is free to carry out its principal tasks of processing and producing information.

Other methods include Mark Sensing, Optical Mark Reading, Magnetic Ink Character Recognition (MICR) and terminals, etc. (*see* IX, **15–21**).

4. Master files. Master files in computer systems are either magnetic tape and/or disc files, containing records relating to employees, sales, purchases, stocks and names and addresses, etc. Such files are the equivalent of ledger cards or loose-leaf records used in manual or mechanised systems.

Magnetic tape files are useful for high capacity, serial access requirements, whereas disc files have the advantage of direct access, which increases processing productivity Disc files, however, are more expensive and have a lower capacity than tape files (*see* IX, **5**).

Computer files in the form of magnetic tapes and discs are the computer's filing cabinet, as they provide high capacity "backing storage" facilities. Due to cost factors, it is not possible to store all records in the processor's internal memory. Instead, records are transferred into the processor's memory when required either for updating or reference purposes (*see* IX, **4**).

MANAGERIAL ASPECTS OF IMPLEMENTING A COMPUTER

5. Planning the use of a computer. When a computer is to be introduced into a business, management is confronted with a number of considerations regarding its effective use. Without doubt, the organisation structure will require changing with the advent of a computer, as many clerical activities and management planning and control functions will be taken over by the computer (*see* VI and **6, 7**).

An initial organisational problem is the structuring of the data processing department in the organisation. A guide to resolving this problem is to establish whether the computer is to be used by several functions, for accounting applications only, or as a dedicated system for a particular purpose.

If it is to be used throughout the business for many functional purposes, then it should be structured as a function in its own right, reporting directly to the chief executive, general manager or administrative director, whichever is most suitable for the circumstances. It is then possible for the data-processing needs of the business as a whole to be co-ordinated, to optimise the use of the computer at corporate level, rather than at functional level.

A steering committee needs to be formulated, whose membership may consist of representatives of the various functions which will be affected by the computer. The committee would, in many instances, be chaired by the chief executive, which would enable him to consider corporate policy with regard to any computer projects which are proposed. He could then indicate whether the projects are compatible with the future strategy and policy of the business.

The interests of functions, in a typical manufacturing environment, could be represented by such functional managers as the production controller, stock controller, chief accountant, sales manager, chief buyer and the data processing manager, etc.

The Steering committee, as a policy formulating body, would be guided in its decisions by defined Terms of Reference. Its duties would be to appraise the viability of projects to ensure that they accord with corporate policy and future developments already under consideration and that they would be of benefit to the business as a whole. The steering committee would also be responsible for controlling the design stage of projects, through project leaders, and reporting to appropriate senior managers to keep them informed of progress. In this way, senior management does not become technically or administratively involved to any great extent. Technical matters are delegated to appropriate specialists and administrative matters to the steering committee.

Senior management should, of course, take an interest in all stages of project development and progress in applications for which they are directly responsible. They need to become conversant with the features of the system and its operating characteristics, so that they have adequate knowledge to effectively control the system when it becomes operational.

The structuring of a computer in the organisation, in the manner indicated, removes the possibility of inter-functional friction, which may arise if data-processing is controlled by a functional manager. Friction may occur if data-processing is controlled by the chief accountant, for instance, who possesses the same level of authority as other functional managers being serviced by the computer.

When computers first came on the business scene, they were often installed to replace punched card installations, controlled by the chief accountant in many instances. Under these circumstances it was a practical arrangement for the chief accountant to be responsible for the computer installation, as it was mainly used for accounting applications. Eventually, as experience was gained in using computers, their usefulness for applications other than accounting was recognised and it was then necessary to re-

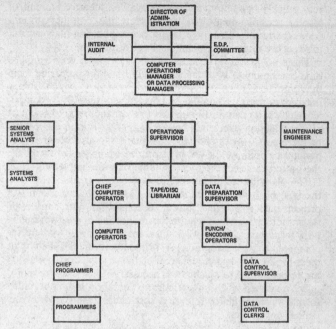

FIG. 29 *Data processing department organisation chart.*

structure the position of the data processing function. Figure 29 illustrates a representative organisation chart of the data processing function.

6. Management planning and the computer. It is, of course, the prerogative of management to decide which of its planning activities should be computerised. The degree of detail involved with specific planning activities may be a deciding factor. Two notable examples are budget and production planning. Budget planning is a very time-consuming activity, because of the large number of variables and constraints which must be co-ordinated to compile the master budget plan. Very rarely is the master budget acceptable to top management on its first presentation, consequently budget amendments are necessary (*see* V, **8, 9**). Such amendments take a considerable amount of time, but they can be processed very quickly by computer, so saving a considerable amount of management planning-time. What is more, the computer can generate a series of alternative budget plans, allowing management to select the most suitable one for implementation.

The preparation of production plans is also a very complex, time-consuming task, which is a good reason for preparing them by computer. When amendments are necessary, which is very frequent in practice, they can be effected very speedily by computer which is a great advantage, because amendments to one part of a production plan often have a chain reaction on other parts of the plan. A series of alternative plans can also be developed perhaps to optimise the use of resources. Management then have the option to select the most suitable plan for implementation.

The planning technique used depends to a great extent upon the type of production undertaken, i.e. whether large, complex projects such as a bridge, power station, ocean liner, tanker, oil rig or motorway, which require the application of a network planning technique. The network plan may be printed out by the computer either as a graph or printed schedule. If batch, or mass-production, techniques are used then a great deal of scheduling of operations to machines is necessary. Linear programming may be applied when an optimisation solution is sought, either to maximise profits or minimise cost, within the framework of defined constraints.

On the other hand, management may wish to use a computer for strategic planning, by means of marketing models for corporate development involving long-term planning, rather than short-term planning.

The availability of a wide range of package programs, covering the whole planning spectrum, simplifies the use of a computer in such cases, since management can assess the characteristics of packages and correlate them with business requirements, as a guide to the selection of appropriate planning activities for computerisation (*see* Table VIII on p. 111).

7. Management control and the computer. It is one thing to plan, it is another to control. Planning without control is ineffective, because there is no provision for management to take corrective action, as circumstances dictate, to achieve the objectives which the plans indicate (*see* XI, **18–23**).

It may, therefore, be accepted that planning and control are complementary. Management then need to consider how best to use the computer for control of business operations. The approach to computer control will necessitate an appraisal of the information-requirements of management in respect of types of report required, the frequency of such reports, degree of accuracy acceptable and the timeliness of such reports. Information requirements must be studied in detail by systems analysts, as new data may need to be generated by the various systems, particularly an integrated information system, to provide for new information requirements. In this respect, it is worthwhile to be aware of the shortcomings of the present systems regarding information flows and reports (see XI, 9–11).

When any system is computerised, it should not merely be a replica of the present system, but should incorporate improvements, particularly with regard to business control. The problem confronting management is to decide how best to use the computer to assist in control activities, whether it is concerned with stock control, credit control, budgetary control or production control, etc.

The manner in which information is obtained is an important factor to consider—it could either be:

(a) Complete print-out of files after computer runs have been completed, which includes the updating of master-files relating to stocks or customers, etc.

(b) Exception reports, including those relating to stocks which require replenishment, customers' accounts which have exceeded credit limits or budget variances, etc.

(c) On-line information retrieval facilities which may be associated with on-line updating systems such as on-line order-entry (see IX, 19, 20).

ESSENTIAL FACTORS FOR THE SUCCESSFUL INTRODUCTION OF A COMPUTER

8. Feasibility study. A computer cannot be "plugged in and away she goes", as it were: its successful implementation depends upon a number of factors and one of the most important of these, if not the most important, is the need to conduct a thorough "in-depth" feasibility study. On the basis of such a study management decides, that is it makes a decision either to use, or not to use, a computer in the business. Whichever decision is made, it can have far reaching effects on the future of the business and its efficiency. The crucial factor is whether the decision is correct, because it is

possible to make an incorrect decision in either of two instances. In the first instance, based on a feasibility study report, management may decide not to use a computer when in fact it should be used, and in the second instance, management may decide to use a computer when in fact it should not be used.

The result of not using a computer, when it should be used, is reduced administrative efficiency. The effect of using a computer, when it should not be used, is chaos, as systems will be disrupted, unnecessary costs will be incurred and organisational changes will be made needlessly.

9. Top management support. The time, effort and finance required for the development of computerised systems may deter the most enlightened management from accepting any proposal to do so, unless the feasibility study report makes refusal difficult. This is another pointer to the value of an accurate feasibility study report. It is, of course, imperative for top management, i.e. the board of directors, to show interest at the outset, otherwise projects will have little chance of success once a computer is installed.

Any dissension on the part of top management will filter through the organisation to the lower management echelons and this, in itself, will detract from the successful implementation of systems. Departmental managers in charge of systems being computerised will not provide the required level of support to the systems staff which is essential for efficient operation of the new systems. User departments need to participate in the design of systems with which they are concerned.

10. Education and training programme. The reason for any lack of management enthusiasm may be ignorance of computers and the benefits which they can provide. This may be resolved by a suitably structured internal education and training programme, conducted by the systems staff. Such a course could include:

(a) Definition of a computer.
(b) The place of the computer in the business.
(c) Duties of systems analysts and programmers.
(d) The responsibilities of the data processing manager.
(e) Outline of computer applications.
(f) Benefits of using computers related to present systems.
(g) Data preparation methods.
(h) Processing techniques—batch, on-line and real-time systems concepts.

As an alternative, or in addition, to internal courses, selected management and staff representatives may attend computer manufacturers' or college-based computer appreciation courses.

11. Communication. When a computer installation is being considered, the fact should be communicated to all personnel, particularly those in the administrative functions, who are likely to be the most affected. Responsibility for this lies with the managing director and, by means of an official communication, he can dispel any rumours at the outset which may have a damaging effect on morale.

It is necessary to communicate company policy with regard to possible redundancies which may occur when work is transferred to the computer. Of particular importance are the arrangements to be made for retraining staff and possible redeployment. The managing director should also state the importance of obtaining the fullest co-operation of staff in the difficult systems-development and change-over phases.

12. Recruitment of effective data-processing staff. An effective Data-processing manager is essential and he should possess a wide knowledge of the business, its policies, organisation structure and systems. Because of this aspect, he is often appointed from within the business, as it is usually recognised that it is easier for him to learn about computers than all the ramifications of the business. The Data-processing manager needs to be a good administrator, in preference to being a computer expert, as he needs to be able to plan, co-ordinate and control projects efficiently. He must, of course, be conversant with computers, particularly with the model in use, but he need not be an expert in programming or systems analysis. He certainly needs to be familiar with such techniques, however, so that he may more easily assess the day-to-day problems being encountered during systems development and data processing. He would, of course, need to attend suitable training courses.

The Data-processing manager is also responsible for interpreting and executing the policy of the steering committee and controlling his staff in the attainment of objectives.

Systems analysts should be recruited from within the organisation, whenever possible, to take advantage of their knowledge of the business, which is of benefit for the development of new systems. Analysts must be aware of the purpose and objectives of the project they are undertaking and have the ability and imagination to recognise and develop new approaches to old problems.

Programmers, particularly when using assembly code (low-level programming language) for the writing of programs, must have an intimate knowledge of the computer which will run the programs, to take account of the machine's characteristics. The more efficiently the programs are written, the lower is the running time on the computer.

13. Systems design. Systems should be designed without unnecessary complexity—the simpler the design, the more effective they are likely to be. User-department staff will understand the systems they are concerned with more easily the less complex they are.

It is good practice for staff concerned with systems which are undergoing investigation for computerisation, to join the study team, to enable their experience to be incorporated in the new systems. The staff will appreciate being invited to participate and the systems are likely to be that much more suitable and effective as a result. Systems should be fully documented, for reference purposes and so as to enable amendments to be effected easily. A high turnover rate often occurs with systems analysts and programmers, due to their search for promotion and development and, consequently, new staff must be provided with a method of learning the details of the systems for which they are now responsible, when the staff who originally developed the systems have left the business (*see* XI, **6, 12**).

14. Systems implementation. Before a new computer system is implemented, it may be necessary to conduct "pilot" runs with test data, to ensure that the system achieves its defined purpose and objectives. Programs must of necessity be subjected to trial runs with test data, consisting of both valid and invalid data, for the purpose of ensuring that the program can contend with all possible eventualities. Corrections are then made, either to the programs or the system, and subjected to further trials (*see* XII, **9**). When the situation appears to be satisfactory, "parallel" running of the new system and the existing system can commence. The results produced by both systems can then be compared and any notable differences investigated and corrected. This is a "fail-safe" procedure, as it would have drastic consequences on the business if the old system was dispensed with before the new system had proved to be adequate. It is not unknown for "bugs" to appear after parallel running has been dispensed with, even after detailed trials have been conducted.

15. Monitoring performance. Computer systems must be monitored to detect any deviations from planned results and performance, so that suitable amendments can be effected and staff subjected to further training if necessary.

16. System updating. The term "system updating", sometimes referred to as "systems maintenance", is the process of ensuring that a system meets current requirements. Systems must be adjusted for the needs of change, either for fundamental reasons, e.g. the introduction of VAT, or for systems development in respect of integration, or the introduction of on-line processing. When packages are used, amendments to programs may need to be effected, perhaps for more efficient running of the relevant programs.

CRITERIA FOR SELECTION OF COMPUTER APPLICATIONS

17. Cost factors. It is often considered that cost savings are an essential requirement for the economic viability of computer applications. Cost savings should be achieved whenever possible and the most usual test applied for this purpose is the comparison of the annual operating costs of the new system, or proposed system, with those of the current system. If the result is not favourable, then a decision may be made not to go ahead with the new system proposal, which may be an erroneous decision. An important factor has been overlooked—the benefits that can be provided by the new system compared with those of the current system. The golden rule to apply is, "if the value of benefits exceed the cost of obtaining them, then it is a viable proposition". In such cases, it is possible to face the increased operating costs without being bothered in the least.

The cost of the current system may be lower than it should be, because it is inefficient and fails to achieve its objectives, e.g. invoices and statements of account may be running several weeks late, resulting in an inadequate cash-flow, which is critical to running the business on a solvent basis.

18. Speed and volume factors. Due to the phenomenal speed with which a computer can process data, a much higher volume can be processed in a specified time than is possible by other methods. In such cases, even though the annual operating costs of a computer application may exceed those of the previous system, the cost of processing each unit of data is likely to be lower. This is particularly important if the previous system was overloaded and if additional staff would be required if a computer was not used to replace the existing manual or mechanised system.

19. Accuracy of information. Management needs information that is reliable for problem-solving and decision-making and this is facilitated by a computer, as error-detection routines are incorporated in computer application programs which are referred to as "validation checks". Examples of validation checks are summarised as follows:

(*a*) Check to ensure that data are of the correct type, in accordance with the application being run on the computer.

(*b*) Check to ensure that the data relate to the correct period.

(*c*) The use of check digits to ensure that correct account, stock, employee and expense codes are being processed.

(*d*) Check to ensure that data conform to the minimum and/or maximum range of values, e.g. stock balances, customer order quantities and values, gross wages and so on.

The objective of a data validation system is to detect errors at the earliest possible stage, before processing commences. It is pointless processing invalid data, as it is a waste of resources. In addition, invalid data can have drastic effects on the business, as it is possible to order ten times the quantity of materials required by the mere insertion of an additional nought in the order quantity. The effect of an error can also be increased when it is subjected to arithmetical calculation, such as when multiplying a quantity by a price.

Sole reliance should not be placed upon a computer for the detection of errors however, as it is important to ensure that data are recorded on source documents as accurately as possible. Similarly, it is important to check the accuracy of data preparation operations, such as punching data into cards, before data are processed, and this is achieved by a punched card verification process.

Information produced by computer can be said to be generally more reliable than that produced by clerical systems, as human fallibility is eliminated to a great extent. Once a program has been written, with appropriate checks incorporated, then the relevant procedure is carried out automatically. A clerk, on the other hand, can have his/her attention distracted by environmental conditions such as the need to answer the telephone or to discuss work

TABLE VIII. PROBLEM SOLVING PACKAGE PROGRAMS

Package	Description and purpose
1. PERT—Program Evaluation and Review Technique	A comprehensive set of inter-linked computer programs dealing with every aspect of network planning and control
2. PROSPER—Profit Simulation, Planning and Evaluation of Risk	Designed for use by corporate planning departments, financial directors and accountants for the construction of financial models May be used for such applications as budgeting and budgetary control, capital investment appraisal, overall corporate planning, cash flow forecasting and pricing of new products
3. PROP—Profit Rating Of Projects	Calculates the net cash flow and after-tax position of a project by consideration of capital investment, cost and income cash flows
4. PROMPT—Production Reviewing, Organising and Monitoring of Performance Techniques	Provides a complete and integrated production control system covering breakdown, stock control, factory planning and control (including forward loading, short-term loading, works documentation, progress control) and purchase control

problems with a colleague. Clerks also can be "off colour" and may not give their work the required degree of concentration when this occurs, consequently errors go undetected in many instances. This is not to say, however, that clerical systems do not have checking facilities: indeed they do, but automatic checking facilities provided by computer programs are generally superior.

20. Problem solving. Although many computer installations are predominantly concerned with processing high-volume, routine data for applications such as payroll and sales ledger, etc., the more advanced installations use the computer as a management tool in the area of problem solving. In this instance, the power of the computer is harnessed to scientific methods of problem solving as practised by operational research specialists.

This development is mainly attributable to the wide range of problem solving package programs which are available for the type of problem outlined in Table VIII.

PROGRESS TEST 8

1. Define the term "computer configuration". **(1)**
2. Outline the basic features of a computer. **(2)**
3. The traditional method of data capture and preparation for processing involves a number of stages. New methods, however, do not necessarily follow a similar pattern. Discuss the implications of shortening or accelerating the cycle, illustrating your answer with examples. **(3)** (I.A.M. W1974, Part A, Q3)
4. The capture of data is often the part of a system most likely to create the greatest problem. Explain some of the problems of data capture by describing three computer applications and the equipment and techniques being developed to minimise the difficulties. **(3)** (I.A.M. S1973, Paper 2, Q7)
5. Input data in a computer-based system are often validated at three stages, viz:

 (*a*) data origination;
 (*b*) data preparation/transcription;
 (*c*) within the computer program.

Describe the needs for validation at each stage and the types of check performed. **(3, 19)** (I.A.M. S1973, Paper 1, Q3)
6. Contrast and compare the use and maintenance of manual records with computer files and show the difference in methods. **(4)** (I.A.M. W1974, Part A, Q8)
7. It is contended that senior management can control the design stage of a computer-based project without becoming too techni-

cally involved. Discuss this view and suggest ways in which management can retain control without full involvement.   (5)

(I.A.M. W1975, Paper 11, Q6)

8. A recently published survey reported that the prime reason for installing computers was to provide a "better service to managers". Discuss the implications of this objective.   (5–7)

(I.A.M. S1974, Part A, Q6)

9. What criteria should be used to assess the suitability and effectiveness of reports generated by an integrated business information system?   (7 and IX, 19, 20)

(I.A.M. S1973, Paper 1, Q5)

10. Early applications of computers were predominantly to be found in areas of accounting and financial control, such as payroll and ledger maintenance. The second phase of applications, however, has moved into integrated information and control systems. Describe the different nature of the analysis and design work in this area.   (7 and XI, 9–11)   (I.A.M. S1973, Paper 1, Q2)

11. State the purpose of a computer feasibility study.   (8)

12. Why is it necessary to obtain the support of top management for the introduction of computer systems?   (9)

13. Why is a programme of education needed within an organisation before a computer is installed? Describe the content that you would desire in such a programme.   (10)

(I.A.M. S1973, Paper 2, Q4)

14. The regular introduction of new techniques and revision of systems may have an unsettling effect upon staff. How may an administrative manager guard against such dangers, yet maintain up-to-date systems which meet the current needs of his organisation?   (11)   (I.A.M. W1974, Part B, Q2)

15. As Office Manager, you have agreed that a systems feasibility study will be introduced into the area within your control. Describe the likely effect of this study upon the morale of your staff, and describe the action you would take to counteract it.   (11)

(I.A.M. S1973, Paper 1, Q6)

16. Suggest and justify the criteria to be used in selecting a member of staff who is to be responsible for the development of computer-based systems in an organisation without previous EDP experience.   (12)   (I.A.M. W1974, Part B, Q1)

17. State the importance of recruiting effective data processing staff when introducing a computer into the business.   (12)

18. State what you consider to be important considerations for the successful introduction of a computer in respect of systems

design, implementation, monitoring performance and system updating.   (13–16)

19. What difficulties are likely to be encountered at the implementation stage of a project? Suggest principles which should be
followed to avoid or minimise those difficulties.   (14)

(I.A.M. W1974, Part B, Q4)

20. What are the advantages and disadvantages of parallel running as compared with the use of test data in the proving of a
computer-based system? What is the role of the user in the former
process?   (14)   (I.A.M. S1973, Paper 2, Q5)

21. By what factors should computer applications be selected?
(17–20)

22. Many writers have proposed that cost saving is neither the
most relevant nor the most important criterion to justify a new
system, whether computer-based or not. Discuss this view and
propose alternative criteria that could be used.   (17–20)

23. How can the reliability and validity of source data be assured
in a computer-based system?   (19)

CHAPTER IX

Computers and Business Systems: Applications and Processing Techniques

DEFINITIONS OF DATA PROCESSING TERMS

Before proceeding with further considerations of computer applications and processing techniques, it is important for the reader to understand a number of basic data processing terms in addition to those already mentioned (*see* VIII, 1–4).

1. Data processing operations. All data processing systems whether manual, mechanical or electronic must be built up from a series of operations. The operations must be arranged in a logical sequence. An operation is usually the smallest identifiable step in a procedure, the performance of which changes the state of data towards the required form.

Typical data processing operations are as follows:

(*a*) Recording data on source documents in respect of business transactions.

(*b*) Sorting data into a logical sequence.

(*c*) Summarising data by classification code.

(*d*) Analysing data by classification code.

(*e*) Merging related data-master records and transaction data.

(*f*) Calculating related data elements, e.g. Quantity × price.

(*g*) Comparing data—actual results with budgeted results or actual results with standards or actual stock quantity with re-order level.

(*h*) Updating records (balances +/− transaction data)

(*i*) Printing results of processing.

2. Source document. This is a document used for the initial recording of data relating to business transactions (*see* 1(*a*)). Typical examples of this type of document are given in Table IX.

For processing by computer the source data indicated in Table IX needs to be converted into machine sensible form (*see* VIII, 3).

TABLE IX. SOURCE DOCUMENTS

Type of document	Data recorded
Despatch note	Items despatched to customers
Time sheet	Time spent on jobs
Clock card	Attendance time
Piecework ticket	Data relating to "payments by results" schemes
Issue note	Issues from stores
Goods received note	Receipts into store
Purchase requisition	Request for items to be purchased
Insurance claim form	Details of claim, e.g. accidental damage to a car
Package holiday booking form	Details of holiday resort and hotel required

3. **Reports.** "Report" is the term used to define the output from a data-processing system, which is normally in printed form. A report is any output, whether basic business documents, schedules or control reports.

(*a*) Basic business documents.
    (*i*) Invoices.
    (*ii*) Statements of account.
    (*iii*) Payslips.
    (*iv*) Purchase orders.
(*b*) Schedules.
    (*i*) List of account balances, either customers or suppliers.
    (*ii*) List of items in stock indicating quantity, value, orders placed, reserves and shortages, etc.
    (*iii*) Company payroll summarising gross pay, tax, deductions and net pay relating to each employee.
(*c*) Control reports.
    (*i*) Age analysis of account balances.
    (*ii*) Cost variance reports.
    (*iii*) Stock items requiring replenishment.
    (*iv*) Product profitability report.

(*v*) Utilisation of resources report.
(*vi*) Insurance claims exceeding specified amounts.
(*vii*) Holiday overbooking report.

4. File updating. Reference has already been made to "records" and "master files" (*see* VIII, 4). The updating of records stored in master files is for the purpose of ensuring that the records indicate the latest information in respect of customer, supplier and stock balances, etc. It is important to appreciate, however, that the information can only be as up to date as the last updating run (*see* 5 and 13).

5. File activity or "hit" rate. The proportion of records updated or referenced on each updating run, in relation to the total number of records on a master file, is referred to as the "hit" rate. This is a very important consideration in computer configuration deliberations, regarding the type of storage media most suitable for specific applications, i.e. magnetic tape or magnetic disc.

In respect of magnetic tape files, it is necessary to access each record on the file serially, even though some of the records are not affected by current transactions. What is more, the whole of the file has to be re-written on to a new tape file. In this case, a file with a low "hit" rate can increase processing time and would be better stored on magnetic disc, which has direct access capability. Direct access requires only those records affected by transactions to be accessed for updating. In addition, records stored on disc do not have to be written to a different disc after updating since records are overwritten.

As a payroll file has a high "hit" rate, there is no advantage in storing it on magnetic disc, as every employee's record needs to be updated each pay period. Magnetic tape has a high storage capacity and is cheaper than magnetic discs. On the other hand, a stock file may contain records which are only affected by transactions occasionally, therefore the whole of the file does not change each time a computer run is made. In this case, processing time can be reduced by storing stock records on magnetic disc.

6. File security. File security is essential in computer systems, as it is possible to overwrite or accidentally erase records stored on magnetic media. The purpose of file security is to provide the means of reconstituting master files when records are corrupted, erased or overwritten in error during processing.

The consequences would be more drastic to a business if the

whole, or even some of its master files were lost than if the computer installation was destroyed. The computer installation could be replaced more easily than the information the files contained. It would be possible to use stand-by facilities to continue processing data during the time required to install a new computer installation (*see* Appendix IV).

Magnetic tape files utilise the "generation" technique of file security, so called because the files of the two previous updating runs are retained, together with the current file. The two previous period files and the current file constitute three generations of files, referred to as Grandfather, Father, Son. The corresponding movement (transaction) files are also retained, in the event that the files have to be re-run to reconstruct a corrupted file.

Magnetic disc files are normally copied to magnetic tape for file security measures. Copying is referred to as "dumping". File retention is not normally applicable to discs because of cost, on the one hand, and the mode of updating on the other. As previously stated, records on disc files are overwritten during updating, destroying the previous records. If a copy had not been produced and corruption occurred during processing, then there would be no basis for reconstructing the file. The file copy is retained until the next dump when it may be used for any required purpose.

7. File reference. During processing it is often necessary to refer to reference files for extraction of data elements required for specific applications. Examples are shown below:

(*a*) *Sales accounting.* When producing invoices or statements, the name and address of the customer requires printing on the documents. Reference to a customer name and address file is made for this purpose.

When preparing invoices, product descriptions and prices are required for each item despatched to customers. In this case, reference is made to a product or commodity file.

(*b*) *Payroll.* When preparing payrolls, it is often necessary to refer to a wage-rate file for the calculation of gross wages. In other instances, the wage rate may be a data element on the transaction file, in which case a reference file is not required.

8. File amendments. File amendments include the addition of new records and the deletion of obsolete records from master files. This is often referred to as file maintenance. Examples of file amendments are:

(a) The addition of new starters and the deletion of terminations from the payroll or employee master file.

(b) Changes of addresses on customer and supplier reference files.

(c) Changes to product prices on the product or commodity file.

(d) Changes to wage rates on the wage rate file.

9. File conversion and creation. When applications are to be transferred to a computer, the master files must be converted from their present form to a computer-compatible form. This means the conversion of records from a visible form, on ledger cards, to an invisible form, on magnetic tapes or discs.

Before conversion, it is necessary to reconcile the balances and other data on existing records, before punching the data of each record into a punched card. This procedure may necessitate punching data elements into a different sequence to that used at present. New code numbers may also be required, in which case the existing codes must be converted to the new codes on the punched cards.

File conversion to punched cards creates a high-volume punching operation and suitable arrangements must be made for this commitment, especially as the cards must also be verified. The actual file conversion is not yet complete, as the cards must be further converted to magnetic media. This is accomplished by transferring the data in cards to the processor by means of a card reader. Card to tape, or disc, conversion is then achieved by a data validation program, already prepared in readiness for processing the transaction data of the relevant application.

During the file conversion run, the new records are printed out and these must be manually reconciled with the old records, to ensure there are no irregularities. All errors must be corrected.

Most files are not static, as variable data are forever changing, due to normal business transactions, and difficulties arise in maintaining files in phase with the manual system files, during parallel running. During this phase, it is necessary to update two sets of files for reconciliation purposes, to ensure that the computer is producing accurate results (*see* VIII, **14** and **19**).

10. Computer run. A run may be defined as a unit of processing consisting of a number of operations or processing steps. Each run is shown on a computer-run chart as an action box (*see* Figs. 30–32). A program is prepared for each run, which is loaded into the computer's internal memory by the computer operator. The computer operator is responsible for setting up each run, as directed by the run chart and operating instructions. The setting up of a run involves the operator in the following activities:

(a) Selecting program from library which may be stored on magnetic tape or disc.

(b) Loading tape to tape drive or, if disc, to disc drive.

(c) Loading program into memory.

(d) Selecting master files from library with regard to the application being run.

(e) Loading tape drive or disc drive, as appropriate, with master file.

(f) Loading card reader, or paper tape reader, with transaction file.

(g) Loading appropriate stationery to line printer.

(h) Loading tape drive with a reel of tape for file updating requirements if appropriate.

As can be seen from the activities indicated above, which describe the typical requirements for batch processing (*see* 13), computer operations require a great deal of operator participation. The operator's degree of involvement has been decreased however, by the technique of multiprogramming (*see* 27–29).

COMPUTER APPLICATIONS AND CHOICE OF PROCESSING TECHNIQUES

11. Applications. In the context of batch processing (*see* 13), a computer application may be defined as a series of related computer runs for a defined purpose, whereby runs are inter-connected by the output from a preceding run providing the input to the succeeding run. Figure 24 indicates the run structure for an order-entry application. Figure 25 outlines the runs for an integrated nominal ledger application.

Additional illustrations of computer applications are shown in Figs. 30–32, which outline the run charts for typical payroll and stock control systems.

12. Choice of processing technique. When an application is being considered for processing by computer, it is necessary to consider which processing technique or techniques will be the most suitable for the needs of the business. The techniques to be applied may be limited by the capabilities of the computer configuration installed, which will have been considered during the initial feasibility study. It is, of course, possible either to enhance the present computer configuration, replace it by a more powerful model, or have an additional dedicated computer system. In the latter case, the present system may be suitable for batch processing requirements, but an additional system may be economically viable for either on-line processing or real-time control needs (*see* **15–26**, and Appendix III).

Factors to consider in the choice of technique are:

(*a*) The suitability of processing data in batches.
(*b*) The need for direct access to information.
(*c*) The need for data transmission facilities.
(*d*) The need to update files by on-line terminals.
(*e*) The need for real-time control of operations.
(*f*) The need for multiprogramming.
(*g*) The need for time-sharing facilities.

BATCH PROCESSING

13. Batch processing defined. The technique of batch processing is widely applied in computer and non-computer data processing systems. It is concerned with processing batches of related data at defined periods of time and stipulated frequency. Batch processing operations relate to specific applications and consist of a number of related computer runs (*see* **4–8, 10, 11** and Table X).

An important feature of batch processing is file updating and in this respect it is important to appreciate that all data (from source documents) and records (from master files) must be resident in the internal memory of the processor before updating is possible. This requires the transfer of data by an input device and records from backing storage devices.

Updated records are then transferred to backing storage, tapes or discs, which are then stored in the library until required for the next updating run. This situation can create problems for dealing with enquiries of a random nature, as files are not accessible until the next run, when the computer is specially set up for a particular application. To deal with enquiries on an individual basis is not economically viable, as it would necessitate the setting up of a run specially for the purpose. If enquiries are sufficiently numerous, however, it may be worth scheduling a special enquiry run to deal with batches of enquiries. In this case, access to appropriate

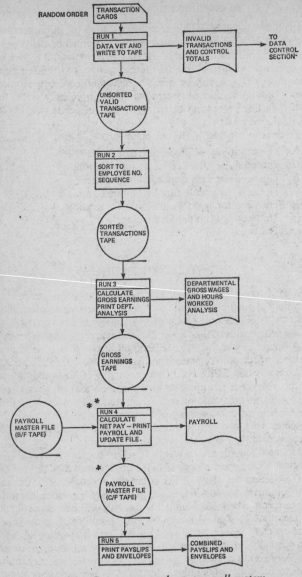

FIG. 30 *Computer run chart—payroll system.*

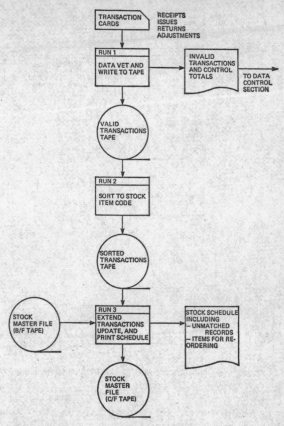

FIG. 31 *Computer run chart—stock control system (magnetic tape).*

records, such as customer or supplier accounts, can be facilitated by an enquiry package program.

Alternatively, if an application is run on a daily basis, then the details printed out of particular records may be adequate to deal with enquiries, therefore avoiding a special run. A 24-hour turn-round time may be suitable in most cases.

When files are permanently "on-line" to the computer, then

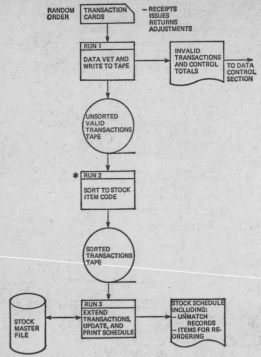

FIG. 32   *Computer run chart—stock control system (magnetic disc).*

access to records for enquiry purposes may be accomplished directly, by an enquiry terminal. The system must be developed for this purpose initially however.

On-line computer enquiry facilities are the counterpart of the direct-access facilities provided by ledger cards and loose-leaf records in mechanised and manual systems. In such cases, all that is necessary to deal with an enquiry is to refer to the appropriate record in the file directly. Such records, of course, can be read by people, whereas computer records cannot.

File updating is performed systematically, at defined periods of time and frequency, depending upon circumstances. With regard to frequency, this is dependent upon the volume of transactions

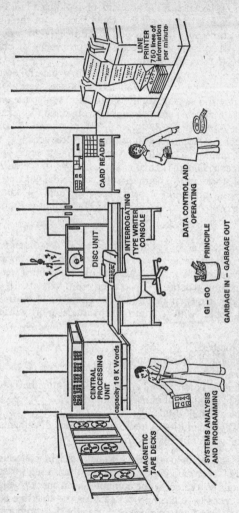

FIG. 33 *Batch processing computer configuration.*

in some instances, because of the necessity of avoiding a build-up of data. Invoices may need updating daily because of the high volume involved, because if it was performed weekly the processing time may be so long as to preclude the processing of other important jobs, the payroll for example.

On the other hand, a particular application may have a "natural" updating frequency. The payroll has a natural weekly updating frequency for a factory payroll and for staff paid on a weekly basis. For monthly paid personnel the updating frequency is monthly.

A further consideration regarding time and frequency, is the importance of management information regarding specific operating requirements. One particular example known to the author is in respect of stock control which is subjected to daily updating, because management require a daily stock schedule for control purposes—the control of stocks being a key factor in the running of the business (*see* IX, 4).

14. Batch control. In order to control the flow of data in and out of the data-processing system, it is normal practice with computer systems to have a batch-control section. The batch-control section receives all incoming data for processing from various departments (user departments) or branches. The data is normally received in batches, with a control slip attached on which is recorded:

(*a*) Batch number.
(*b*) Department or branch number.
(*c*) Batch control data:
    (*i*) Document count (number of documents in the batch).
    (*ii*) "Hash" total (total of account numbers).
    (*iii*) "Meaningful" totals:
      —Total of quantities of items on individual documents.
      —Total value of transactions.

A "Hash" total refers to a total which has no significance apart from being useful for data control purposes and is used for comparing the totals generated by the computer, as a check to ensure that all documents have been processed. It is possible that some documents may have been overlooked during the data preparation stage and not presented for processing.

Each batch of documents is recorded in a register indicating the date when the batch was received. The batches are also scrutinised for obvious errors before being despatched to the data preparation section.

The punched cards or paper tape prepared in the data preparation section provide the batches in machine-sensible form, for processing by computer. The batches are processed in accordance with pre-defined runs (*see* 10).

After processing, the batches of documents and the printed output from the computer are sent to the batch-control section, where they are entered in the register as a record that all batches have been processed. The output is checked for errors and corrections are made by user departments. The corrections are presented for processing either as separate batches, or included in batches to be processed during the next period.

The reader may wish to refer once again to Figs. 24, 25, 30–33 for examples of batch processing applications and a typical batch processing configuration. The definitions of data processing terms are also relevant to batch processing and the reader is recommended to refer once again to 1–10.

REAL-TIME PROCESSING

15. Definition of real-time processing. Some businesses, or parts of a business's operations, are dependent on up-to-date and relevant information being available on request for efficient operation and this is often facilitated by computer based real-time systems.

The term "real-time" refers to the technique of updating files with transaction data, on such a time-scale that the operation to which the transactions relate can be controlled effectively. This is in distinction to "batch-processing", which processes batches of data at pre-defined periods. "Real-time" processing is a concept rather than a particular method of processing, so that the use of a computer is not automatically implied. If a perpetual inventory technique is applied to a clerical stock control system, whereby all transactions are recorded immediately they occur, rather than at defined periods of time, then in effect, it is a real-time system.

This type of system, however, may have a slow "response-time" in the provision of management information, and the updating process may be slow due to the volume of transactions involved. Therein lies some of the reasons why a computer is necessary, particularly as some types of business have dispersed operations, such as airlines with dispersed booking offices. Such real-time systems must be communications-oriented whereby the

geographically-dispersed units are connected to the remote computer by communication lines and terminals. These facilities are
essential for on-line updating of information files and dealing
with random enquiries on an interactive conversational basis (*see*
Fig. 34).

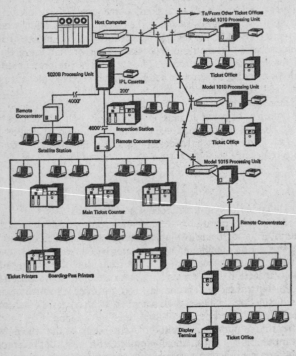

FIG. 34   *Typical airline reservations and ticketing system.*

On occasions, computers are dedicated to real-time operations
and one such instance is real-time control of steel-making, which
has been researched specially for this book (*see* Appendix III).

16. Dual purpose computers. Other computer configurations are
designed to operate in both batch and real-time mode. The Singer
System Ten is a small computer with this capability, whereby up
to 20 operations can be handled concurrently. Input/output ter-

minals can be situated over 500 m from the central processor, enabling various departments in a company to be on-line to the processing facilities by means of strategically sited work stations (conversational, typewriter or interactive VDU terminals, etc.). By means of these facilities it is possible to process invoice data and payroll data, etc., concurrently. A remote job-entry facility is also available (*see* 21).

For real-time requirements, the system provides a fast response to requests for information and processing requirements. Up to 20 such requests can be entered simultaneously by means of local and remote communication facilities. This is possible by means of a partitioned internal memory.

17. Operating system. All computers are controlled by software, known as an operating system, and in respect of a combined batch and real-time configuration, the operating system provides interrupt facilities to deal with real-time requirements, either for updating or information retrieval. The interrupted batch program is transferred to backing storage and the program required for the real-time operation is called into the processor's memory. After dealing with the real-time updating or enquiry, the interrupted program is transferred from backing storage to internal storage and processing is recommenced from a "re-start" point. All this takes but a few seconds.

18. Comparison of batch and real-time systems. Master files containing operating information are normally stored on magnetic disc and need to be permanently on-line to the computer, both for updating and retrieval requirements. With batch-processing operations, the master files are stored off-line until required for a specific application.

Real-time processing also attempts to process each transaction through all the relevant steps at one time whereas batch processing processes all transactions through specific steps before proceeding with other processing steps. This is in accordance with the structure of batch processing runs.

In addition, real-time systems are dynamic as they accept random transaction types at random time intervals, consequently the status of file contents change dynamically. It is this characteristic which makes it difficult to audit or recover the system in the event of system failure. Both of these factors are facilitated by means of periodic check points, say every 2–3 minutes, at which all relevant restart and audit information are dumped to magnetic tape. These dumps can be used to restart the system and assist auditing activities.

Another feature of real-time systems, contrasted with batch processing systems, is the reduction in the volume of print-outs, as most information is displayed on a VDU screen in a transitory manner. This, and other, contrasting features of batch and real-time systems are shown in Table X.

TABLE X. COMPARISON OF BATCH AND REAL-TIME SYSTEMS

Batch	*Real-time*
1. Routine high volume applications —Invoicing —Payroll —Sales ledger updating —Stock ledger updating —Nominal ledger updating	1. Business control applications —Steel making —Stock control —Airline operations and aircraft seat reservations
2. Data collected for a defined period of time and processed in batches.	2. Data input at random intervals as events occur.
3. No direct access to system by user departments.	3. Direct access to system by on-line terminals by user departments.
4. Files only on-line during a processing run.	4. Files permanently on-line.
5. Magnetic tape files may be used for sequential access to records. Disc files may be used as an alternative.	5. Direct access disc files usually used.
6. Information on the files is only as up-to-date as last run.	6. Information on files constantly up-dated as events occur.
7. Detailed reports and transaction lists printed.	7. Most information is displayed on a VDU screen as messages. Alternatively may be printed on a teletype.
8. Audit trails facilitated by means of transaction lists and	8. Audit trails not so well provided for, as control is

TABLE X.—*cont.*

Batch	Real-Time
contents of files printed by means of an audit package.	centred around the number of messages input rather than details of transactions.
9. All transactions recorded on source documents prior to input in machine-sensible form.	9. Transaction details input by terminal keyboard, sometimes from source documents, sometimes not, depending upon the system.
10. Information from computer files only accessible during a specially set-up run.	10. Information permanently available on demand.

ON-LINE PROCESSING

19. Definition of on-line processing. The term "on-line" relates to terminal-based computer operations whereby terminals are connected to, and controlled by, a remotely located processor. On-line systems at present are being developed for a wide range of applications in different types of industry, including banking, building societies, tour operators and stock exchanges, etc. Figure 35 outlines an on-line computing system used by tour operators, whereby reservation offices spread throughout the country accept telephone input from travel agents and other booking agencies enquiring about the availability of holidays for clients. Immediate file access is available through the VDU screens to the local operator and a holiday booking can be checked and immediately booked. Similarly, Fig. 36 outlines an on-line computing system used by stock exchanges, whereby terminals are located on the floor in major stock exchanges throughout the country and in participating brokerage firm offices. Such a system provides the means of communicating with the computer-based order processing and communication system.

A distinction requires to be made between "real-time" and "on-line" processing. "Real-time" systems process transactions in a time-scale that permits the effective control of business systems, which enables them to optimise their performance. Computer-based, real-time systems are of necessity on-line systems, as ter-

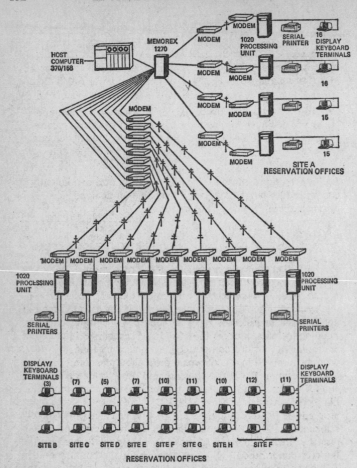

FIG. 35.   *On-line computer system—tour operators.*

minals connected to a remote processor are a basic characteristic
of such systems. On-line systems are not necessarily real-time systems however, as they are sometimes used as a more efficient
alternative to batch processing. In this case, instead of preparing
data in a machine-sensible form for processing in batches at pre-

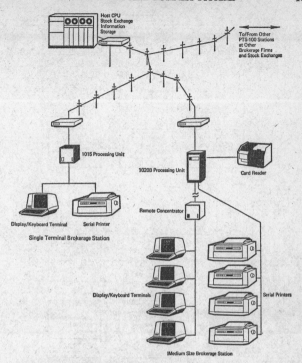

FIG. 36 *On-line computer system—stock exchanges.*

defined periods of time, input of transaction data is effected by terminal at random time intervals.

In addition to the types of system indicated above, which are specific applications in different industries, on-line facilities are also a feature of other processing techniques including data collection systems and time sharing (*see* **22–26**).

20. On-line order-entry system. There now follows an example of an on-line order-entry system, which is based on information supplied by the Patent Shaft Steelworks Ltd. The application is concerned with processing stock and rolling orders received by the steelworks and an outline of the present system is shown in Fig. 37. A feasibility study was undertaken to justify the merits of on-line

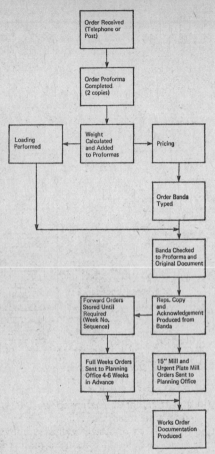

FIG. 37   *Outline of clerical order processing system.*

processing compared with batch processing. On-line order-entry was justified after considering the following factors:

(*a*) *Stock orders.* Low demand situations lead to customers (stockholders and users) holding low stocks, consequently they require rapid deliveries. The ability to transmit orders directly to despatch locations helps to achieve this.

(b) *Rolling orders.* Low demand situations again mean that orders taken today may be for rolling tonight. A batch system will always result in some orders not getting through due to validation checks. An on-line system provides on-line validation and consequently all orders get through allowing the mill to continue rolling.

Applying the batch processing technique, the sales department would be required to record on an order proforma the account number, number of units, dimension, codes in respect of quality, specification and additional instructions. The proforma would

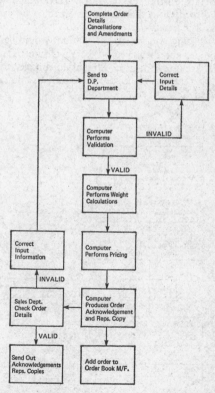

FIG. 38   *Batch processing order-entry system.*

then be passed to the data processing department for punching in readiness for processing by computer. The remaining information requirements in respect of customer names and addresses, qualities and loading instructions, etc. would be obtained from master files.

The computer would then perform input validation checks, weight calculations, pricing, order acknowledgment and the addition of the order details to the order book master-file. The sales department would then check the order details and correct invalid data for reprocessing (*see* Fig. 38).

Applying the on-line processing technique the typist would type the order details on the keyboard of a VDU which would enter the details directly into the computer. In this way each entry is validated as it is typed.

Loading, pricing and weight calculations would be performed by the computer and displayed on the VDU screen, as the typing of the order progresses. An additional advantage would be the display of each customer's credit status and an "index of profitability" for each order.

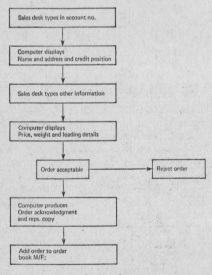

FIG. 39   *On-line order-entry system.*

The correction of invalid coding would also cease to be a problem, as the computer would check each item of data as it is entered by the VDU.

The order book master-file would be used to produce works order documentation when required, thereby eliminating some routine clerical work. It would also be used for providing answers to one-off queries and for use in production control activities.

On-line processing would reduce the punching load in the data preparation section and provide a faster response to pricing and weight queries that arise as a result of telephone enquiries. Weight, pricing and loading details would also be available the moment the input of order details was completed (*see* Fig. 39).

21. Remote job entry. This is an on-line processing technique whereby remote locations equipped with data transmission facilities are able to transmit data to a central processing installation. The data is then processed and the results may either be transmitted back to the remote location and printed on a local printer, or the print-outs may be produced at the computer installation and sent by post or messenger service.

The technique is referred to as "remote batch processing" or "remote job entry" which enables batch processing to be employed by operating units which do not have a computer installed locally but share the use of a computer on a group basis. Such facilities are also available from a number of computer bureaux which provide time-sharing services. In this case a user may develop a program by time-sharing terminal and then get it run over-night on a batch basis by bureau staff (*see* **23–26**).

22. On-line data collection. Such systems are used for the speedy collection of data from dispersed locations, to provide management information for business control. Strategically-sited transmitting units are connected to a centrally located computer, for transmitting data for processing and file updating. A notable example of on-line data collection is in respect of a factory data-collection system, which enables data in respect of manufacturing operations to be speedily collected for production control purposes.

Two types of data have to be collected, i.e. fixed and variable. Fixed data may be pre-punched on punched cards, or embossed on plastic badges similar to the Access card which, in respect of manufacturing data, may typically include; order number, week number, operation number and part number. Variable data, in respect of manufacturing operations, may typically include employee number and the quantity produced. This data is recorded by means of a keyboard, levers or dials on an input unit.

Data recorded on punched cards are transmitted to the computer, by inserting the cards in a slot on the transmitting unit and depressing a "transmit switch".

Data recorded on plastic badges are transmitted when these are inserted into a badge-reader. Data represented by dial or lever settings are transmitted by the depression of a "transmit switch".

TIME-SHARING

23. Definition of time-sharing. Time-sharing is the term used to describe the service which places a computer at your finger tips, by means of a remote computer, located at a computer bureau, which is available to many users on a multi-access basis. The effect is such that each user is unaware that the computer is being used by other users and this creates the impression of having a computer available for one's sole use. The use of a computer in this way enables computer power to be utilised by many more users than would otherwise be economically viable, as it is not necessary to incur the costs and problems associated with installing a in-house computer.

24. Interactive processing. Time-sharing facilities provide an interactive conversational mode of processing, with instant response from the computer to questions asked or statements made by the user. It is this feature which facilitates the work of accountants, corporate planners and managers concerned with business planning activities and problem solving, as results may be obtained, using appropriate models of business activities and relevant programs, in a much shorter time period and at lower cost than is possible by normal methods of calculating. The results obtained are used as the basis for establishing corporate plans and decision-making, which greatly improves the effectiveness of business operations and profitability.

25. Access to computer. Access by each user to the remote computer is accomplished by means of a terminal unit, which may either be a tele-typewriter, which is a machine similar to an electric typewriter, or a visual display unit similar to a television screen. The terminal may be connected to any ordinary telephone extension line by means of a modem or acoustic coupler rented from the Post Office. A modem, or acoustic coupler, is an item of equipment connected to each terminal in a communications complex, using telephone lines. It is necessary to have a modem or acoustic coupler, as telephone lines transmit data in the form of analog signals and data terminals transmit signals in digital form and the device is used for converting digital signals to analog signals and vice versa. The term "modem" is a contraction of "modulator" and "demodulator". The terminal can be located in the office environment wherever there is a telephone extension.

The telephone handset is used for establishing a link with the remote computer and, when not in use for this purpose, it may be used for normal calls. When a user has established contact with the computer, it is necessary to key-in the user's identification number on the keyboard of the terminal unit. The computer responds by requesting the user's password, which is keyed-in on the terminal's keyboard but is not printed for security purposes. This procedure is to ensure that only personnel authorised to use the facilities can gain access to the computer files. After keying-in the correct password, the user keys in the code for the specific program he wishes to use for model building or problem solving. The appropriate program is loaded into the computer's internal memory to enable processing to commence. The user then enters the data to be manipulated, by means of the terminal keyboard. The responses and results from the computer are printed out on the user's tele-typewriter or, when using a visual display unit, they are displayed on the screen. When processing is concluded, it is necessary for the user to log-out from the system.

The computer, because of its high processing speed, powerful operating system and extensive file storage capacity, can share its time between many terminals, switching from one to the other at high speed without any apparent delay to any user.

26. Problem solving. A very important factor of time-sharing is that users do not need a detailed knowledge of computers, programming or mathematics for problem solving. Problem solving is facilitated by means of application programs, which incorporate numerical methods appropriate to solving the various types of problem of the user, e.g. discounted cash flow, sales forecasting, sensitivity analysis, critical path analysis and linear programming etc.

MULTIPROGRAMMING

27. Definition of multiprogramming. A small computer installation may process one program at a time and find this quite adequate for its processing load. In such instances, the running of the application programs is controlled by a basic control program such as ICL 1900 series, Executive.

Eventually, as more applications are transferred to the computer, it may be found that there is insufficient processing capability, operating on the present basis of one program at a time. Multiprogramming may then need to be considered, whereby two or more programs can be processed concurrently. This enables overall processing time for all programs to be reduced, even though the time required to process individual programs may be increased, due to switching between programs. Such operations are still controlled by the basic control program, but the computer operations staff are responsible for determining the program mix, that is, the programs which are to be run together, and the order in which they are to be run. This is referred to as work-scheduling and in a large installation it becomes a complex and time-consuming task. Therefore, as the purpose of multiprogramming is to increase the utilisation of the computer system as a whole, there is a need to employ more powerful software, in the form of an operating system incorporating automatic work-scheduling features. A programmer may then specify scheduling factors in a "job description", which allows the operating system to perform work-scheduling activities automatically. A "job description" specifies the name of the job, the peripherals (input and output devices) required, priorities, the streams of data to be input and output and the time programs take to run.

28. Mode of operation. Multiprogramming operates in the following way—when processing is interrupted on one program, perhaps to attend to an input or output transfer, the processor switches to another program. This enables all parts of the system, the processor and input and output peripherals to be operated concurrently, thereby utilising the whole system more fully. When operating on one program at a time, the processor or peripherals would be idle for a large proportion of the total processing time, even though this would be reduced to some extent by buffering. Buffering enables the processor to execute another instruction whilst input or output is taking place, rather than being idle whilst the transfer is completed. Even so, when processing one program at a time, basic peripherals are used for input and output, such as card readers and line printers which, being mechanical, are slow compared to the electronic speed of the processor and this causes imbalance in the system as a whole.

29. Off-lining. Multiprogramming employs the technique of "off-lining", which requires the transfer of data from punched cards (or paper tape) to magnetic media, such as discs, before programs are run. Similarly, output from some programs would also be output to magnetic media for printing, when the printer becomes available. In this way, it is possible to process the payroll and prepare invoices by loading both programs into the main memory. While the line printer is printing an invoice line, the processor switches to the payroll. Afterwards, the processor reverts back to the invoice application. As the printer is being used for printing invoices, payroll data would be recorded on magnetic media for later conversion when the printer is available.

PROGRESS TEST 9

1. Define the following data processing terms:
   (a) Processing operation
   (b) Source document
   (c) Report
   (d) File updating
   (e) File activity or "hit" rate
   (f) File security
   (g) File reference
   (h) File amendment   (1–8)

2. Information files are generally the hub of any system. Discuss the principles that should be followed in their design and use. (4–8, 18 and VIII, 4)   (I.A.M. S1975, Paper A, Q3)

3. Given the fact that most files in organisations are not static, describe a programme for file conversion to a computer-based system, including the requirements for such a programme and the detailed procedure.   (9)   (I.A.M. S1974, Part B, Q3)

4. Discuss the major operations and detailed planning involved in the setting up or conversion of file data prior to the implementation of a computer system.   (9)

(I.A.M. W1975, Paper 11, Q1)

5. Define the term "computer run".   (10)

6. When an application is being considered for processing by computer it is necessary to consider which processing technique is likely to be the most suitable. Indicate the factors to consider in the choice of technique. **(12)**

7. Define the term "batch processing". **(13, 14)**

8. One of the major problems of introducing computer-based batch processing systems is in providing a satisfactory service to deal with enquiries. Enlarge upon the problem and propose measures to minimise the difficulties, highlighting the implications of your proposals. **(13)** (I.A.M. W1974, Part B, Q3)

9. Describe how enquiries may be dealt with in a computer-based batch processing system, e.g. an enquiry relating to a customer account. How satisfactory is this process likely to be as compared with a typical manual or mechanical processing system? **(13)** (I.A.M. S1973, Paper 1, Q4)

10. The factors of timeliness and accuracy of data may be regarded as being inextricably linked. Discuss the considerations affecting a systems designer in relation to these factors, and provide examples of different uses of data to illustrate your answer. **(15 and VIII, 19)** (I.A.M. W1973, Paper 1, Q1)

11. Define "real-time" processing. **(15–18)**

12. Contrast batch and real-time processing. **(18)**

13. Are computer or manual methods more likely to fulfil the purpose and objectives of systems? **(15)**

14. In what ways and to what extent will the use of a terminal as part of a multi-access computer system assist the clerical functions of an organisation? **(15, 16, 19–22, 25)**

(I.A.M. S1973, Paper 2, Q3)

CHAPTER X

Analysis and Development of Clerical Systems

THE NATURE OF ORGANISATION AND METHODS

1. Organisation and methods defined. Organisation and Methods is a specialist activity performed by O. & M. investigators, which attempts to improve the efficiency and effectiveness of clerical systems by the most suitable means. This is achieved by conducting detailed analytical studies of the present systems, to establish problem areas and their causes, as a first step to their improvement.

O. & M. investigators are impartial observers, free from departmental considerations, and are therefore able to view situations objectively—they are able to see the wood *and* the trees, as it were. Departmental managers on the other hand may not be able to see the wood for the trees, as they are fully engaged with their normal operating responsibilities. In addition, departmental managers may not foresee the need for change for the purpose of improving the efficiency of the operations for which they are responsible, due to over-familiarity. From the foregoing, it can be seen that an independent assessment of systems is essential, hence the reason for using specialist O. & M. staff.

2. Advisory function of O. & M. O. & M. investigators act in an advisory capacity to functional and departmental management and their staff. Accordingly, they do not have executive authority over any staff in areas where they are conducting investigations.

O. & M. staff are invited to carry out investigations in specific departments by the appropriate management, for the purpose of advising them on problems associated with office layout, form design, work allocation, work simplification and alternative methods, etc.

3. Attributes of O. & M. staff. It is essential for O. & M. staff to have the widest possible knowledge of business systems, preferably gained in conducting investigations in several businesses. By this means, it is possible to compare current situations with previous situations, which can aid the formulation of solutions to problems. Seemingly similar problems may require an altogether different approach to their solution however, so O. & M. staff need to avoid the danger of applying ready-made solutions to problems. Investigators must have an enquiring mind, tact, patience, impartiality, originality and tenacity. They must also be courteous when conducting assignments and never overlook the fact that they are dealing with people, especially when conducting interviews for collecting facts.

4. Objectives of O. & M. In general the objectives of O. & M. are to improve the effectiveness of clerical systems, as stated above, by simplifying and eliminating unnecessary operations. Individual Terms of Reference for specific assignments indicate specific objectives to be attained which may include:

(*a*) Improve supplier relations by more effective ordering procedures.

(*b*) Improve customer relations by more effective order handling procedures and dealing with enquiries more efficiently.

(*c*) Improve manpower utilisation.

(*d*) Reduce work cycle time.

(*e*) Reduce the level of errors.

(*f*) Improve the forms in use so that they take less time to compile.

(*g*) Simplify the methods in use.

(*h*) Streamline the organisation structure of specific departments.

(*i*) Integrate defined procedures.

(*j*) Standardise specific operations or methods.

(*k*) Eliminate work duplication.

(*l*) Reduce operating costs by the most suitable means.

(*m*) Utilise office space more effectively.

(*n*) Reduce the time necessary to perform defined operations.

5. Selection of projects. Projects are often selected on the basis of "key factors", in order to obtain the greatest benefits, as it is a means of concentrating investigations on important elements of systems. A procedure with a high incidence of errors can have repercussions on both internal and external business activities. Also, the cost of finding and correcting errors may be a high proportion of the operating costs of the system and, accordingly, improvements should aim at reducing the level of errors and the incidence of checking.

Systems with a high volume of documents, forms and reports to process, relative to other systems, offer good prospects of cost savings, and a speedier flow of work, if documents and forms which no longer serve a viable purpose are eliminated. Improved methods of processing may also be developed, providing additional benefits.

Systems with a large number of operations offer greater scope for improvement, either by eliminating operations altogether, or by combining related operations to avoid unnecessary duplication of recording of similar data on different documents.

The manpower element of systems should be investigated, because systems with a large number of personnel have high payroll costs and occupy a large proportion of the total office space. It may be found that more personnel are employed on activities than is really necessary, because of low efficiency or inadequate allocation of tasks and supervisory control. The application of work measurement techniques combined with work simplification may well justify the costs associated with such studies.

6. Preliminary survey. A preliminary survey is carried out in the area of the proposed assignment, in order to become familiar with the operational environment and to obtain first impressions of the activities performed. Such a survey is concerned with the following factors:

(*a*) Discussing the problem areas with the appropriate functional management, supervisors and staff.

(*b*) Examining the forms and documents, the layout of the office, the machines and equipment in use, and the flow of work.

(*c*) Examining any procedure manuals in existence to establish whether they are out of date or, if they are up to date, whether they are being adhered to.

(*d*) Clarifying whether the department or system under review has to conform to any specific policy considerations.

(*e*) Determining the purpose of the work performed, the objectives that must be attained, the types of problem that need to be solved, the investigations that appear to be necessary and the sequence in which they should be conducted.

(*f*) Deciding the relationship of the area to be studied with other operating areas and systems and the likely effect of changes upon them.

(*g*) Assessing the amount of time required to conduct all stages of the investigation.

(*h*) Determining the number of O. & M. staff required on the various stages of the assignment.

(*i*) Agreeing the initial terms of reference with the projects committee and functional management.

7. Terms of reference. The terms of reference constitute the authority for conducting the assignment and they should preferably be in writing, to avoid ambiguity and misunderstanding. They are usually agreed during the course of the preliminary survey and should be prepared on the basis of the factors indicated below:

(*a*) The purpose and objectives of the area to be investigated must be clearly defined.

(*b*) The areas and boundaries of the assignment must be defined.

(*c*) The functional heads in charge of systems effected by the assignment must be specified for liaison purposes.

(*d*) The priority rating of the project must be established so that its relative importance to other assignments is known.

As investigations proceed, it may be necessary to modify the terms of reference as new factors come to light, as it may be appropriate to pursue the project beyond the initial boundary lines to deal with matters affecting related systems.

COLLECTING THE FACTS

8. Examining the existing situation. Collecting facts is the stage in an assignment concerned with the examination of existing operations, procedures and systems in order to understand how they work, the elements that comprise them, the resources they use, their effectiveness, problem areas and the cost of operating them. This is a very important and necessary part of an assignment and the efficiency with which it is performed will have a bearing on the ultimate improvements which are developed and implemented.

This fact-finding activity may be defined as "systems analysis", and before proceeding with a detailed examination of a system, it is useful to be aware of the environment in which the system operates, to enable a wider appreciation to be obtained before modifying the system concerned. Features of importance include the type of business activity, its products, markets, organisation structure and where the system fits into the overall scheme of things.

9. Facts required about systems. The basic facts required may be obtained while interviewing operating personnel, or by observing activities. In general, when asking questions during fact finding interviews, a series of questions may be framed in the following manner:

What is it that is done?
Why is it done?
When is it done?
How is it done?
Where is it done?
Who does it?

Specific facts may be obtained by first drawing up a check list covering the important elements of systems as outlined below.

(a) *Resources used.*
    (i) Machines and equipment.
    (ii) Number of personnel employed.
    (iii) Office space occupied.
    (iv) Type and volume of forms and documents.

(b) *Operating data.*
    (i) The point of origination of documents.
    (ii) The operations performed at each work station.
    (iii) The flow of documents between work stations.
    (iv) The movement of personnel between work stations.
    (v) The type of master records and files used.
    (vi) The details contained in the master records and files.
    (vii) Specimens of completed documents, forms, schedules and reports.

(c) *Quantitative data.*
    (i) Details of volume of activity—smallest, average and largest number of documents processed during each operating period.
    (ii) Processing cycle times for individual operations or for completing documents or reports.
    (iii) Frequency of reference to files.
    (iv) Distances of movement of both forms and personnel.
    (v) Time spent on work discussions.
    (vi) Time spent on telephone.
    (vii) Time spent using machines and equipment.

(*viii*) Time spent in setting up machines for processing operations.

(*ix*) Time spent on machine maintenance.

(*x*) Proportion of time machines are idle due to no work or being out of order.

(*d*) *Qualitative data.*

(*i*) How efficiently the work is performed.

(*ii*) The type, frequency, importance and reason for errors.

(*iii*) Problems caused by errors.

(*iv*) Condition of records.

(*v*) Condition of machines.

(*vi*) Adequacy of working conditions for type of work done.

(*e*) *Effectiveness of present procedure.*

(*i*) Average backlog of work.

(*ii*) Average cost of performing operations.

(*iii*) Number of hours of overtime worked.

(*iv*) Cost of activity compared with budget.

(*v*) Efficiency of staff.

(*vi*) Effectiveness of staff allocation.

(*vii*) Suitability of forms and reports for their purpose.

(*f*) *Organisation structure.*

(*i*) The functional manager responsible for the procedure or system under review.

(*ii*) The manager's immediate subordinates and span of control.

(*iii*) Supervisors' subordinates and span of control.

(*iv*) Job titles of personnel.

(*v*) The main activities of each section.

(*vi*) The effectiveness of delegation.

(*vii*) The extent of any duplication of activities.

(*g*) *Policy matters.* It is essential for O. & M. investigators to be aware of any policy matters concerned with specific activities and whether they are being applied, understood and administered correctly. Unfortunately, many policies are not in writing, which creates the possibility that they may not be passed on to successors in positions of responsibility, who have the duty to conform to such policy. Whenever any policy is amended, it should be communicated immediately to all those concerned with its implementation. Otherwise, operations may be geared to the achievement of outdated objectives.

(*h*) *External influences.* External factors, often generated by government legislation, have effects on internal systems, for example, changes in national insurance rates, VAT rates, inflation, metrication, International Standards Organisation paper sizes and Post Office Preferred envelope sizes have far-reaching effects on systems. All matters of this type must be checked to ensure that systems accord with such requirements whenever necessary. Of course, such changes generate special projects for their implementation or revision, which is one of the reasons for the constant need for change to ensure that systems are geared to current, rather than historical, needs.

RECORDING THE FACTS

10. Recording techniques. Having collected a host of facts on the present system, an investigator must now marshal the facts into some logical order for further appraisal. Any O. & M. investigator should be fully conversant with the most widely-used recording techniques and be able to evolve special techniques as the need arises.

The most frequently used techniques for recording facts are procedure narratives, procedure analysis charts and activity lists.

11. Procedure narrative. This is a written description of a procedure or system which is prepared on the framework indicated below:

(a) Title of the procedure or system.
(b) The purpose of the procedure or system.
(c) The principles governing the procedure or system.
(d) The departments concerned with the procedure or system.
(e) The activities performed by each department.
(f) The forms used in the procedure or system.
(g) The reports produced by the procedure or system.
(h) The machines, equipment and other resources used.

It is normal practice to supplement a procedure narrative with pictorial representations of procedures or systems, by means of various types of chart. It is difficult to grasp the detail of systems from written descriptions alone, as one of the important requirements is to clearly appreciate the logical relationships between various activities. By means of references to specific charts in the procedure narrative, a deeper understanding is facilitated and the characteristics of systems are more easily apparent.

PROCEDURE: Sales ledger (conventional accounting machine)	CHARTED BY	R.G.A.	REF. No.
DEPARTMENT: Sales accounting	DATE	28/5/77	
FORM: Ledger card and statement	SHEET NO.	1 of 1	
CHART BEGINS: Enter address on statement	CHART ENDS	Post statements to customer	

SUMMARY

SYMBOL	ACTIVITY	PRESENT	PROPOSED	DIFFERENCE OR SAVING
○	OPERATION	11		
□	INSPECTION	1		
⇨	TRANSPORT	–		
D	DELAY	–		
▽	STORAGE	1		
	TOTAL DISTANCE			
	TOTAL TIME			

Activity Number	DETAILS OF PRESENT METHOD	Operation ○	Inspection □	Transport ⇨	Delay D	Storage ▽	Distance	Time	POSSIBILITIES: Eliminate	Combine	Separate	Improve	CHANGE: Simplify	Sequence	Place	Person	Method	Form	NOTES
1	Enter address on statement	●							√								√		For each account at the beginning of
2	Transfer balance outstanding	●							√								√		each month
3	Select ledger card and statement to be posted	●																	Repeat for each ledger
4	Compare address on ledger card with address on statement		●						√								√		Card to be posted - activities
5	Pick up and insert carbon paper	●							√								√		3 to 11
6	Align statement and ledger card for posting	●							√								√		
7	Insert into the accounting machine	●																	
8	Post entry	●																	
9	Withdraw ledger card and statement from machine	●																	
10	Remove carbon paper	●							√								√		
11	Re-file ledger card and statement					●													
12	Extract active account statements from file	●																	End of month
13	Post statements to customer	●																	End of month

FIG. 40 *Procedure analysis chart—present procedure (sales ledger accounting machine system).*

			REF. No.

PROCEDURE: Sales ledger (dyeline process)
DEPARTMENT: Sales accounting
FORM: Translucent ledger sheet
CHART BEGINS: Select ledger sheet

CHARTED BY R.G.A.
DATE 1/6/1977
SHEET NO. 1 of 1
CHART ENDS: Post statements to customer

SUMMARY

SYMBOL	ACTIVITY	PRESENT	PROPOSED	DIFFERENCE OR SAVING
○	OPERATION	11	7	-4
□	INSPECTION	1	.	-1
⇒	TRANSPORT	.	.	
▽	DELAY	.	.	
▽	STORAGE	1	2	+1
TOTAL DISTANCE				
TOTAL TIME				

Activity Number	DETAILS OF PROPOSED METHOD	Operation ○	Inspection □	Transport ⇒	Delay ▽	Storage ▽	Distance	Time	Eliminate	Combine	Separate	Improve	Simplify	Sequence	Place	Person	Method	Form	
									POSSIBILITIES										
										CHANGE								
1	Select translucent ledger sheet to be posted	●																	Repeat for each ledger sheet to
2	Insert into the accounting machine	●																	be posted – activities 1 to 5
3	Post entry	●																	
4	Withdraw ledger sheet from machine	●																	
5	Re-file ledger sheet					●													
6	Extract active ledger sheets	●																	End of month
7	Copy active ledger sheets by dyeline process – (statement)	●																	End of month
8	Re-file ledger sheets					●													End of month
9	Post statements to customer	●																	End of month

FIG. 41 *Procedure analysis chart—proposed procedure (sales ledger dyeline process).*

12. Procedure analysis chart. A procedure analysis chart is widely used for analysing and defining each type of activity. The chart utilises the five basic symbols for describing the nature of each activity in a procedure (*see* Appendix II). Each activity is classified by making a mark under the appropriate symbol, the marks are then joined together by drawing a connecting line and it is then possible to observe the pattern of various types of activity. This type of chart may be used for recording either the present or proposed procedure (*see* Figs. 40 and 41).

The advantages of charts may be summarised as follows:

(*a*) May be prepared more quickly than written descriptions of procedures and systems.

(*b*) The facts are conveyed more meaningfully.

(*c*) Provide a more effective means of comparing present and proposed procedures.

(*d*) Provide greater impact.

(*e*) The basic symbols used for the preparation of charts are readily understood.

(*f*) Activity relationships are clearly seen.

ACTIVITY LIST — MACHINE

PERIOD OF STUDY: 4 WEEKS x 5 DAYS x 8 HOURS = 160 HOURS   MACHINE : ACCOUNTING
DATES OF STUDY : 1st MAY, 1977 TO 29th MAY, 1977   LOCATION: GENERAL OFFICE

ANALYSIS CODE	TIME ANALYSIS / ACTIVITY	Productive Time Hours	Ancillary Time Hours	Operating Time Hours	Idle Time Hours	Available Time Hours	Percentage of Total Hours		REMARKS
1	PAYROLL — MONTHLY, WEEKLY	20					12.5		Total Productive Time = 68.8%
2	STOCK RECORDS	25		80		110	15.6	50.0	
3	SALES LEDGER	20					12.5		
4	PURCHASE LEDGER	15					9.4		
20	MAKE-READY TIME		15	30			9.4	18.8	
21	PUT-AWAY TIME		15				9.4		
30	SCHEDULED BREAK PERIODS				10		6.2		Total Unproductive Time = 31.2% No Maintenance Contract
31	MAINTENANCE TIME				20	50	12.5	31.2	
32	OTHER IDLE TIME				20		12.5		
	TOTAL HOURS	80	30	110	50	160	100.0	100.0	

STUDY PERFORMED BY:

FIG. 42   *An analysis of machine activity.*

13. Activity lists. Activity lists may be used for a variety of purposes, depending upon the characteristics of the procedure or system under consideration. Such lists are used when it is necessary to know the time factor associated with different activities. In this way, it is possible to collect important facts about personnel and machine operations. Fig. 42 illustrates an analysis of machine activity, which clearly shows the time spent on various activities, make-ready time and maintenance time, etc.

VERIFYING AND EXAMINING THE FACTS

14. Verifying the facts. Having collected and recorded the facts, the O. & M. investigator must ensure that they are relevant, accurate and represent the true situation. He should substantiate the facts by reframing questions to which he has previously obtained answers and note any important differences in the answers obtained.

The investigator may enlist the assistance of operating staff by requesting them to check his procedure analysis charts and activity lists to ensure their completeness, validity and accuracy. Verification has the following advantages:

(a) Establishes the reliability of the facts.
(b) Pinpoints omissions.
(c) Eliminates misinterpretations.
(d) Indicates factors requiring further investigation.

15. Examining the facts. Examination of the facts is concerned with a reassessment of all the elements of a procedure or method embracing the following factors:

(a) Unnecessary functions.
(b) Unnecessary levels of accuracy.
(c) Unnecessary variations and complexities.
(d) Unnecessary duplications of data, operations and reports.

DEVELOPING ALTERNATIVE PROCEDURES OR METHODS

16. The approach to development. Having verified and examined the facts systematically and critically, the O. & M. investigator must apply all his skill, knowledge and expertise in the development of ways and means for improving individual operations, procedures, systems or methods. He must consider a number of alternatives, so that he is able to present proposals with confidence, knowing that he has considered all relevant possibilities.

17. The simplification approach. Very often procedures and systems produce the desired results, but not in the most efficient or economical manner. In such circumstances improvements may be achieved by considering:

    (*a*) Re-design of forms to simplify their use and preparation.
    (*b*) Elimination of unnecessary forms and reports.
    (*c*) Separation of complex operations.
    (*d*) Simplification of methods used.

CHOICE OF ALTERNATIVE PROCEDURES OR METHODS

18. The selection approach. In order to select the most suitable method from a series of alternative methods for a specific activity, the investigator needs to consider the relative merits of different classes of machine and be able to compare important factors to aid him in his choice. This is where the investigator needs to draw on his background knowledge initially, before supplementing it with specific information obtained from manufacturers' brochures. It is also worthwhile attending demonstrations of particular machines or visiting offices in which they are in operation, in order to obtain first hand impressions.

19. Mechanical accounting machine versus visible record computer. Although we are in the era of electronic data-processing, mechanical accounting machines, although to some extent superseded by visible record computers, are still widely used. They are used in accounting systems for posting transactions to ledgers. It is therefore advantageous to know the broad characteristics of visible record computers to assess those which differ from mechanical accounting machines. The differing characteristics may be summarised as follows:

    (*a*) Electronic speed of operation compared with mechanical speed.
    (*b*) Increased internal storage capacity.
    (*c*) Increased level of automatic operation because of more powerful programs, use of magnetic ledger cards and peripheral devices for automatic input and output.

(*d*) Electronic calculating facilities.

(*e*) Quieter in operation.

(*f*) Greater degree of systems integration possible, mainly due to programming facilities and magnetic ledger cards.

20. Visible record computer versus main frame computer. For the purpose of comparing the characteristics of these classes of machine it may be accepted that a visible record computer (VRC) is a small machine, whereas a main frame computer is a larger machine. In this instance the characteristics of a visible record computer which differ from those of a main frame computer may be summarised as follows:

(*a*) Does not require a critically controlled environment.

(*b*) Highly trained operators unnecessary as the main requirement is an operator skilled in the use of a keyboard.

(*c*) Lower cost of machine.

(*d*) Smaller internal storage capacity.

(*e*) Programs not usually developed by user programmers but by manufacturer.

(*f*) Less powerful.

(*g*) More flexible in use as it may be plugged into any office power point.

21. Computer bureau versus in-house computer. A computer bureau provides computing services which may be used in certain circumstances as a viable alternative to operating an in-house computer. In this instance, the broad factors to consider in terms of a computer bureau may be summarised as follows:

(*a*) Costs incurred only for services used.

(*b*) Avoids capital outlay for the purchase of a computer.

(*c*) Avoids the need to employ computer operators, analysts and programmers, etc.

(*d*) Enables computer power to be used when volumes of data are insufficient to warrant an in-house computer.

(*e*) Loss of control of turnround time (the time it takes from supplying input data to obtaining printed output).

(*f*) No direct experience gained by internal personnel in the use of computers.

(*g*) Confidentiality of information foregone to some extent, although the code of conduct of bureaux is such that it is mandatory for them to accept the Code of Practice of COSBA—The Computer Services and Bureaux Association.

Similar comparisons to those indicated above need to be made for other classes of machine under consideration, for example, mail room equipment, duplicators and photocopiers, etc. Of course the depth of detail will be more than that outlined, which is merely to indicate how alternative methods may be compared by taking into account relevant factors and the characteristics of the various machines.

Figures 40 and 41 outline sales accounting procedures for the preparation of ledger cards and statements of account. Figure 40 indicates the present method using an accounting machine and Fig. 41 the proposed method using the dyeline process. It can be seen that the dyeline process reduces the number of operations required from eleven to seven. The details shown on the procedure charts indicate how this is achieved.

IMPLEMENTATION

22. Recommendations. Before implementation of a new method, it is necessary for an O. & M. investigator to obtain acceptance of his recommendations—this is a selling job. He should first discuss recommendations informally with departmental heads, supervisors and staff concerned with the proposed changes. If necessary, he should arrange demonstrations of the new ways and means and emphasise the benefits to be obtained from the proposals. After initial discussions a formal written report should be presented to all concerned and there is no doubt that it will be more readily understood than if it had been presented prior to informal discussions and demonstrations.

23. Planning implementation. This involves the preparation of a time schedule for implementing the accepted recommendations. This to a great extent is dependent upon the complexity of the proposed changes, which may necessitate a gradual change-over from the previous procedure or method, with different dates for the various sections or departments concerned. Network planning techniques may be utilised for planning the changeover as the logical stages are then more readily apparent.

Sometimes a pilot scheme may be appropriate, when proposed changes affect several parts of the business. In such cases, the best course of action may be to implement the changes in one section of the business initially and observe the results obtained, before proceeding with implementation on a wider basis.

If a change-over is from a clerical or mechanised procedure to a computer, then it is advisable to run the two systems in parallel and compare the results obtained from the new system. In this way, it is possible to detect and rectify faults before the system "goes live". It is fatal to dispense with the previous system prematurely, because this may result in system-failure, with its consequences. It is not usually possible to revert back to the previous system once it has been dispensed with.

FOLLOW-UP

24. Maintaining contact. After the procedure or method has been implemented and has become fully operational, the staff responsible for the supervision of the installation must maintain contact with the O. & M. department for a while. How long this should be depends upon the prevailing circumstances. However, once the procedure or method is running smoothly, and achieving its purpose and objectives, then this is indicative that no further contact is necessary until the system is due to be updated for new changes taking place in the business.

25. The purpose of a follow-up period. The relevant factors may be summarised as follows:

(a) To ensure that the procedure or method has been installed satisfactorily.

(b) To ensure that new procedures are being adhered to.

(c) To remove the cause of problems which may arise initially.

(d) To instruct staff regarding factors which are not clearly understood.

(e) To make modifications which prove necessary.

(f) To measure results achieved with those expected.

PROCEDURE MANUALS

However well new, or revised, procedures and methods are verbally communicated to operating staff during the period of training preceding the implementation of the changes, it is advisable to have written procedural instructions, formally outlining the purpose, objective and steps involved. There is then no need for doubt in respect of the action to be taken within prescribed circumstances.

26. Advantages of procedure manuals. These are summarised below:

(*a*) Facilitates training of existing and new staff.

(*b*) Assists staff during the implementation period.

(*c*) Provides continuity in the correct performance of a procedure in circumstances of staff turnover, etc.

(*d*) Promotes uniformity of understanding.

(*e*) Provides a basis for revision of procedures.

(*f*) Assists O. & M. investigations as details of the present procedure are already available.

27. Disadvantages of procedure manuals. These are summarised below:

(*a*) Unless updated as changes are effected, they become obsolete and worthless.

(*b*) Considerable time and cost may be incurred in maintaining them in an up-to-date condition.

(*c*) Unless prepared by skilled personnel they may not be readily understood.

28. Conclusion. In conclusion it can be seen that there are a number of stages necessary for conducting O. & M. investigations which are summarised below:

(*a*) Selection of projects for investigation.

(*b*) Preliminary survey.

(*c*) Agreeing terms of reference.

(*d*) Collecting the facts.

(*e*) Recording the facts.

(*f*) Verifying and examining the facts.

(*g*) Developing alternative procedures and methods.

(*h*) Choice of alternative methods.

(*i*) Planning implementation.

(*j*) Implementation.

(*k*) Follow-up.

PROGRESS TEST 10

1. "Organisation and Methods is a specialist activity which aims to improve the efficiency and effectiveness of clerical systems by the most suitable means." Discuss this statement. **(1)**

2. Why is O. & M. an advisory function? **(2)**

3. What knowledge, skills, and attributes are desirable in staff

engaged in the development of administrative systems? **(3)**

(I.A.M. S1974, Part B, Q5)

4. Compile a list of possible O. & M. objectives. **(4)**

5. Projects are often selected on the basis of "key factors" in order to obtain the greatest benefits. Indicate what you consider to be "key factors". **(5)**

6. What is the purpose of a preliminary survey? **(6)**

7. What is the purpose of providing "terms of reference" to O. & M. investigators before the commencement of an assignment? **(7)**

8. Since the analysis stage of a project is the foundation on which design can be built, it is a critical factor in eventual success. Discuss this point of view and propose methods of analysis aimed at achieving maximum effectiveness. **(8–15)**

(I.A.M. W1974, Part B, Q8)

9. Indicate various approaches which may be used for developing alternative procedures or methods. **(16–18)**

10. Many organisations use visible record computers either as a first step towards full computer use, or because of the nature of their data processing work. Outline the facilities offered by VRCs and point out the particular features which attract user organisations. **(19, 20)** (I.A.M. S1974, Part A, Q8)

11. Outline a number of important considerations for establishing whether a computer bureau, as opposed to an in-house computer, will best suit the needs of a business. **(21)**

12. Indicate important factors in respect of systems implementation and follow-up after implementation. **(22–25)**

13. What do you regard as the key factors in the implementation of a new information system? How would you organise and control implementation to ensure adequate treatment of these factors? **(22, 23)** (I.A.M. W1973, Paper 2, Q7)

14. How useful are procedure manuals to systems analysts? Describe the tasks of the analyst and the contribution of procedure manuals to each task. **(26, 27)**

(I.A.M. W1973, Paper 2, Q8)

CHAPTER XI

Analysis and Development of Computer Systems

THE NATURE OF SYSTEMS ANALYSIS

1. Definition of systems analysis. It is an activity concerned with collecting, recording and analysing facts in respect of existing operations, procedures and systems. The purpose is to obtain sufficient knowledge of the present systems to enable computerised systems to be designed and implemented (*see* X, 8).

Possibly it would be more appropriate to classify systems analysis as systems design, because the analysis of systems is only a means to an end. Systems analysis and design are two distinct activities, concerned with introducing a computer system. Figure 43 serves to illustrate the 12 stages of introducing a computer

FUNCTION OF:—

	SYSTEMS	PROG-RAMMING	OPERATING & PUNCHING	CONTROL SECTION
1. SYSTEMS INVESTIGATION	●			
2. SYSTEMS ANALYSIS	●			
3. SYSTEMS DESIGN & SPECIFICATION	●	+		
4. SPECIFICATION REVIEW	+	●		
5. PLANNING	+	●		
6. FLOWCHARTING	+	●		
7. CODING		●		
8. COMPILATION		●	+	
9. TESTING	+	●	+	
10. DOCUMENTATION OF PROGRAM	+	●	+	+
11. LIVE RUNS			●	●
12. MAINTENANCE OF SYSTEM	●	+	+	+

(● DENOTES MAIN RESPONSIBILITY)
(+ DENOTES SOME INVOLVEMENT)

FIG. 43. *Stages of introducing a computer system.*

system, clearly indicating where the stages of systems analysis and design slot in to the overall scheme.

2. Systems analysis and O. & M. analysis. The term "systems analysis" was coined when computers came on to the business scene, and refers to the fact-finding activities prior to introducing a computer. O. & M. investigators also perform systems analysis in the course of systems development, but are not usually called systems analysts, as this term is usually reserved for staff concerned with computer systems. The main difference between the two is one of objective rather than of principle. Whereas O. & M. analysis is concerned with improving existing systems and methods by the most suitable means, systems analysis has the objective of designing effective computerised systems, incorporating improvements superior to those capable of being attained by other methods.

Computerised systems require supporting clerical operations for those activities concerned with recording transactions on source documents, data control and data preparation, etc., so there exists a need for both types of analyst. Indeed, a high degree of co-operation is necessary from personnel engaged on this activity, i.e. O. & M. analysts and systems analysts. On the other hand, all the systems within a business are not computerised for various reasons, e.g. insufficient volume of data for processing to warrant a computer or the reduction in processing time is insufficient to justify the use of a computer.

3. The systems analyst. The systems analyst must have many talents, particularly a wide breadth of business experience, as he must be capable of viewing the business as a total system and yet be able to analyse it into its constituent elements (sub-systems) and observe interrelationships. He must be able to appreciate the interactions which are likely to take place between subsystems, due to taking various courses of action. In addition, he must appreciate external environment influences on internal systems and be able to analyse any part of the business in depth. The attributes and knowledge required by a systems analyst may be summarised as follows:

(a) Varied business background.
(b) Wide knowledge of the business in which employed.
(c) Decision making processes.
(d) Information and control theory.

(e) Office machinery.

(f) Forms design.

(g) Computers.

(h) Accounting and other business systems.

(i) Effective salesman.

(j) Good communicator.

(k) Good listener and interviewer.

(l) Enthusiastic.

(m) Writing competence.

(n) Critical ability.

(o) Tenacity.

(p) Capacity of deductive and inductive logic.

(See VIII, 12).

4. Systems analysis team. Depending upon the complexity and type of system to be investigated, some projects require a team of analysts. It is good policy to recruit suitable personnel from existing staff as it is important that they should possess a sound knowledge of the business.

The team should also include representatives of the various departments of the organisation that will be affected by the investigation. This approach ensures that personnel with an intimate knowledge of the systems being reviewed for computerisation have the opportunity to record facts which may otherwise be overlooked and which are important for the effective design of the computer system (see VIII, 13).

During the course of an investigation, facts have to be collected and analysed in respect of:

(a) Organisation structure.

(b) Policy matters.

(c) Audit and legal requirements.

(d) Information flows.

(e) Volume and frequency of providing reports, number of copies and distribution.

(f) Exceptions to normal events.

(g) System control requirements.

(h) Types of decisions to be made.

SYSTEMS DEVELOPMENT (SYSTEMS DESIGN)

5. O. & M. and systems analyst approach compared. The development or design stage of a project differs greatly, because the

O. & M. analyst may need to assess the viability of applying a particular method to the system under review. He needs to consider workable alternatives for producing invoices, updating the sales ledger, and integrating stock control, for instance. This leads to consideration of the viability of manual methods compared with the possibility of utilising a visible record computer, or computer bureau, etc. On the other hand, however, he may only be concerned with redesigning forms or the layout of the office.

A systems analyst, on the other hand, will be concerned with developing a computerised system, but even so he has in some cases, depending upon the computer configuration available, or which could become available, alternative techniques to consider, e.g. on-line, real-time or batch processing.

6. Objectives of systems design. The design of a computer-based system (and any other type of system) is a creative task, which has as its objective the implementation of a system superior to any possible alternative. Such systems must be designed so that basic business documents and reports are produced in the most effective manner.

Provision should be made for automating decisions of a routine nature whenever possible, which may then be incorporated into the computer program for a specific application. This has the effect of freeing management from making this class of decision and, as a result, leaving more time for non-routine problems and decision making.

Systems should not be designed in isolation from other systems, as many are interrelated, as previously stated, either by the need for basic information or by the output from some systems being the input to others. The processing requirements of the total system—the business—should be considered, even though it may be decided to design separate systems—"sub-systems"—initially (*see* VI, 1–4).

7. Essential factors for the effective design of computer systems. A well-designed system should take into account the following factors:

(*a*) Production of the desired information, at the right time, in the right amount, with the desired level of accuracy and in the form required at an economical cost.

(*b*) Incorporation of checks and controls which are capable of detecting and dealing with exceptional circumstances and errors (*see* XII, **11**).

(*c*) Need to minimise the cost and time spent on recording, data preparation and processing (*see* VIII, **3**).

(*d*) Effective safeguards for the prevention of fraud (*see* XII, **11**).

(*e*) Effective security measures in order to avoid loss of data stored in master files (magnetic media) (*see* IX, **6**).

(*f*) Efficient design of documents and reports.

(*g*) Efficient design of computer runs (*see* **8**).

(*h*) Design of suitable coding systems to aid identification, comparison, sorting and verification of records.

(*i*) Policy matters and their effect on business systems.

(*j*) Legislation and its effect on business systems.

(*k*) Procedures for handling exceptions to normal situations. (*See* VIII, **14**).

8. Design of computer runs. A computer run has already been defined (*see* IX, **10**). When designing a computer application, the number of operations performed in each run should be as high as possible, to avoid too many runs which occupy valuable set-up time. The factors outlined below have a bearing on the constituent elements of each run.

(*a*) The size of core store and the capacity available for storing the program related to a run.

(*b*) The feasibility or desire to segment programs, for overcoming the non-availability of core storage for storing complete programs, by storing segments in direct access backing storage until required for processing.

(*c*) The number of tape decks, disc drives or printers required in a run, which is constrained by the number of such devices available.

(*d*) The complexity of the run in respect of the number of different activities to be performed within the run.

THE APPROACH TO THE EFFECTIVE DESIGN OF SYSTEMS

9. Input to output versus output to input approach. Systems are very often designed from the input to the output stage, whereby data is subjected to processing operations to produce output in the form of documents, schedules and reports. This may appear to be quite a logical course to follow, but the disadvantage is that the output produced may fall short of that which is really required. The reason for this is that output can only be produced from the data available for input. Therefore, if certain information is needed, requiring data not generated by the system, it cannot be provided.

It is more appropriate to approach systems-design from the output to input stage, by first deciding on the output requirements, and then ensuring that relevant data is generated for processing to enable the desired output to be produced. This approach requires not only a detailed analysis of routine print-out requirements but also the information needs of management.

10. Management information approach. The details to be outlined are related to those indicated above (*see* 9). Systems are often designed for routine administrative purposes, rather than for management information purposes. This situation may require a reappraisal of priorities—e.g. which should come first—routine business documents, or information for decision making and control? Obviously, the routine administrative activities of a business must be provided for, as no organisation can operate without records of transactions and basic documents in the form of pay-slips, orders and invoices, etc. On the other hand, effective management of a business relies on efficient control of operations and making the right decisions at the right time.

It must be appreciated that to supply management with its complete information needs may be too costly, so it is necessary to compromise, by supplying what is considered to be essential information for decision making. Effective decisions may be made in this way, providing management appreciate that information is missing and assess the risk factors inherent in making a decision on this basis.

Systems design taking the management information approach may be based on three philosophies:

(a) Databank philosophy (*see* VII).
(b) Systems approach philosophy (*see* VI).
(c) Combined databank and systems approach philosophy.

The latter may be defined as a "decisions-based systems approach" which provides for decision making and information retrieval.

11. Top-down versus bottom-up approach. Many management information systems are computer orientated because of the

computers speed of operation which enables vast volumes of data to be processed more efficiently in a given time than other methods (*see* VI, **6**).

Two approaches may be considered in the design of such systems:

(*a*) *Top-down approach.* Top management require information related to strategic aspects of business, rather than detailed statistics relating to the operation of functions and departments. An overall appreciation of such activities is sufficient to direct their attention to key factors, which may require a modification of strategy and general business policy.

One approach is to design top-level systems for this purpose initially and then build a hierarchy of systems downwards, to provide for functional and departmental operational needs. Systems are usually developed from the reverse direction, to serve the operational needs initially (*see* (*b*) below).

(*b*) *Bottom-up approach.* The operating level of management require detailed information in respect of the activities for which they are responsible for control purposes. Most systems are implemented at this level, as data flows and relationships are more clearly defined. The information needs of top management are then extracted, or filtered, from the functional files to provide the key factors they require for strategic decisions. The advent of the database provides the means of catering for all information needs, at whatever level, but the initial development of a database must first specify the information needs of all levels of management.

NOTE: Considerations of systems implementation, monitoring performance and system updating are referred to in VIII, **14, 15** and **16** respectively.

SYSTEMS SPECIFICATION

12. Purpose of a systems specification. The systems analyst, having developed a computer-based system, must specify in writing the features and operating requirements of the application. Initially, it is presented to management for their scrutiny and approval, prior to implementation. The document also provides a programmer with the details he requires for writing the programs for each run. It also provides formal documentation for system updating and general reference. It is the counterpart of a Procedure manual prepared by O. & M. staff (*see* VIII, **13** and XII, **11**).

13. Structure of a systems specification. A typical systems specification may be arranged into six sections as follows:

(*a*) *Introduction.*

    (*i*) Terms of reference.

    (*ii*) Objectives.

    (*iii*) Expected benefits.

    (*iv*) Annual operating costs, development costs and annual equipment costs.

(*b*) *Systems definition.*

    (*i*) Written description of system embracing clerical and computer procedures.

    (*ii*) System flowcharts, procedure analysis charts and computer run charts.

(*c*) *Equipment.*

    (*i*) Schedule of equipment required to operate the system, including ancillary equipment for data preparation.

    (*ii*) Possible alternative equipment.

(*d*) *Detailed specification.*

    (*i*) Input specification and layout.

    (*ii*) Output specification and layout.

    (*iii*) File record specification.

    (*iv*) Source document specification and layout.

(*e*) *Program specification.*

    (*i*) Details of test data and testing procedures.

    (*ii*) Checks and controls.

(*f*) *Implementation.*

    (*i*) File conversion.

    (*ii*) Parallel running and pilot schemes during program and system testing (*see* VIII, **14**).

    (*iii*) Preparation of job procedures for user departments.

    (*iv*) Preparation of job procedures for data preparation and computer departments.

14. System flowchart. This type of chart is designed to illustrate the flow of documents around the computer and the processing performed by the computer. Some essential aspects of its construction include:

(*a*) The name of each department concerned with the system is recorded along the top of the flowchart.

(*b*) Inputs to the system are shown on the left-hand side of the chart.

(c) Outputs from the system are shown on the right-hand side of the chart.

(d) Processes are shown by the appropriate symbol in the relevant column and contain a reference code.

(e) Each symbol contains a brief description.

(f) Symbols are connected by lines and arrows (see Fig. 44).

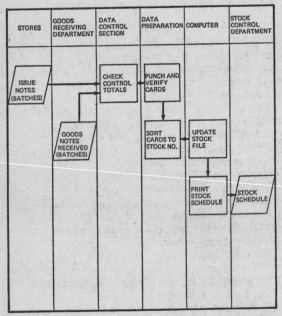

FIG. 44 System flowchart.

15. Computer run chart. Computer run charts are prepared from the systems flowchart and show the sequence of computer operations to be performed (see Figs. 30–32).

DECISION TABLES

16. Use and construction of decision tables. Decision tables are a useful aid to systems analysts for the preparation of complicated flowcharts, as they are used for analysing the factors involved in a problem. They are used for defining conditions that arise in a processing routine and the actions to be taken when the various conditions arise. By this means, it is ensured that a program contains instructions for all relevant conditions and actions, enabling the branching to various parts of the program to be effected, whenever specific conditions are encountered.

A decision table is divided into four parts:

(a) Condition stub
(b) Condition entries } condition statement
(c) Action stub
(d) Action entries } action statement

The condition stub and condition entries define the conditions to be tested. The action stub and action entries define the actions to be taken dependent upon the outcome of testing. The "rules" consist of a set of outcomes of condition tests, together with the related actions.

RULES	RECEIPT	ISSUE	ORDER	POSITIVE ADJUSTMENT	NEGATIVE ADJUSTMENT
	1	2	3	4	5
CONDITION STUB	CONDITION ENTRIES				
TRANSACTION — RECEIPT?	Y	N	N	N	N
TRANSACTION — ISSUE?	–	Y	N	N	N
TRANSACTION — ORDER?	–	–	Y	N	N
TRANSACTION — POSTIVE ADJUSTMENT?	–	–	–	Y	N
TRANSACTION — NEGATIVE ADJUSTMENT?	–	–	–	–	Y
ACTION STUB	ACTION ENTRIES				
ADD TO STOCK	X			X	
DEDUCT FROM STOCK		X			X
ADD TO QUANTITY ON ORDER			X		
DEDUCT FROM QUANTITY ON ORDER	X				
ADD TO STOCK AVAILABLE			X	X	
DEDUCT FROM STOCK AVAILABLE		X			X

FIG. 45 *Limited entry decision table.*

A decision table may be prepared from a procedure narrative (written description), by underlining all conditions present with a solid line and all actions with a broken line. The conditions and actions are then recorded on the decision table.

17. Types of decision table. There are two types of decision table; limited entry and extended entry.

(*a*) *Limited entry*. The features of a limited entry table are:

(*i*) Each condition and action stub contain a limited entry, that is to say an entry complete in itself.

(*ii*) The entry part of the table in respect of the condition stub indicates if a particular rule satisfies the condition.

(*iii*) The entry part of the table in respect of the action stub indicates the action required in respect of the condition entry.

(*iv*) Three symbols are used in the condition entry part of the table; Y (yes), if the condition is satisfied; N (no), if the condition is not satisfied; – (dash), if the condition is not relevant to the rule.

(*v*) In the action entry part of the table, an X is recorded to

RULES	1	2	3	4	5
CONDITION STUB	\multicolumn{5}{c}{CONDITION ENTRIES}				

TRANSACTION	RECEIPT	ISSUE	ORDER	POSITIVE ADJUSTMENT	NEGATIVE ADJUSTMENT
ACTION STUB	ACTION ENTRIES				
ADD TO STOCK	X		-	X	
DEDUCT FROM STOCK		X			X
ADD TO QUANTITY ON ORDER			X		
DEDUCT FROM QUANTITY ON ORDER	X				
ADD TO STOCK AVAILABLE			X	X	
DEDUCT FROM STOCK AVAILABLE		X			X

FIG. 46 *Extended entry decision table.*

signify a required action. If no action is required, the column is left blank (*see* Fig. 45).

(*b*) *Extended entry.* The difference between this type of table and a limited entry table is that the stub parts of the table are not complete in themselves. It is necessary to consider together both the stub and entry parts to determine whether a condition or action is relevant to a specific rule (*see* Fig. 46).

CYBERNETIC CONCEPTS APPLIED TO BUSINESS SYSTEMS

18. Definition of cybernetics. The term cybernetics is derived from the Greek word Kubernētēs, which may be translated as "helmsman" or "controller". It may be interpreted as "the science of communication and control in human and machine systems". In general, the cybernetic control process is identical to the elements of exception reporting (*see* Table XI). Specific terms are used in

TABLE XI. COMPARISON OF TERMS USED IN CONTROL SYSTEMS

Terms used in exception reporting	Cybernetic terms
1. Setting of plans, objectives or standards	Reference input or parameter
2. Collecting and recording facts of actual results of system being controlled	Measurement of output signal by a sensor (a mechanical, electronic or manual data recorder), i.e. measuring the controlled variable
3. Comparison of plans, objectives or standards with actual achievements and establishing variances (deviations)	Comparison of reference input with controlled variable by means of a comparator (an automatic device in a machine, a series of computer instructions or a clerk in a control system)
4. Communication of variances to appropriate manager or supervisor responsible for effecting corrective action	Communication of error signal to effector to adjust the controlled variable to achieve the reference input

cybernetics, however, and the basic terms forming the framework of cybernetics are outlined in Table XI.

A systems analyst needs to be familiar with cybernetic concepts, as many of the systems with which he will be concerned will include control factors, either as the basis of exception reporting or automatic decision making.

19. Cybernetic concepts. When outputs from a system are detected, they are measured by a sensor which indicates the actual state of the system, i.e. measuring the magnitude of the output signal—the controlled variable. The output signal is then communicated by the process of feedback to the control mechanism or device, which includes a comparator. The comparator compares the actual state of the system with the desired state—the reference input or parameter. The difference between the two states is a measure of the variance or error. The error is signalled (communicated) to the effector, a manager or supervisor in the case of a business system, or an automatic device in a machine system, in order to adjust the controlled variable (the input to the physical system) to achieve the reference input and obtain a state of homeostasis (*see* **21**). Figure 47 outlines the concepts in respect of production and production control, whereby the output from the production system is measured and compared with the production target. The difference, or deviation, is either an excess or shortfall of production, which is communicated to the effector, probably the production manager, for corrective action. In some instances, it may be appropriate to modify the system objectives if the initial objectives prove impractical for any reason. Production targets may have been set too high or too low for instance.

20. Feedback. As stated above, feedback is the communication of a systems-measured output to a comparator, for the detection of variances (errors). There are two types of feedback—negative and positive. Negative feedback applies to most business control systems, as they are "negative" error-actuated systems, whereby the actual state of a system is compared with the desired state, and the difference detected as a positive variance (error). Action is then effected in the opposite direction to counteract it.

With regard to positive feedback, the characteristics of some types of system are such that the detected variances require to be amplified. For example, a small manual force applied to aircraft controls is detected and amplified by servo-mechanisms to the force necessary to adjust the control surfaces. If this action was

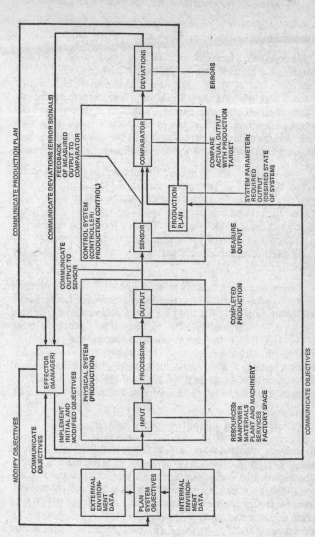

FIG. 47 *Closed-loop production system illustrating cybernetics principles.*

taken in business systems, errors would be amplified and cause the system to deteriorate until it went out of control.

21. Homeostasis. Homeostasis may be defined as the process of balancing or holding steady the parameters essential for the effective control of systems despite buffeting. In a stock control system, abnormal variations in demand and supply are disturbances to normal behaviour, causing buffeting. In such cases, stock control parameters, such as the level of safety stock, may overcome such disturbances. However, it may sometimes be necessary to modify all the relevant parameters to allow for changing trends.

22. Noise. Noise is the term used to indicate the presence of unwanted signals in communications which causes the required signal to differ from that transmitted. As the effective control of business operations is dependent upon accurate information, the incidence of noise is likely to distort the information received by the controller or effector. Consequently the state of a system may be misinterpreted and incorrect action taken to remedy the situation.

23. Redundancy. Redundancy refers to the addition of characters to ensure that information is received correctly, for example, the spelling-out of a value, in addition to presenting it in the normal way, i.e. £50 (fifty pounds). The element of redundancy is often incorporated into communications to overcome the problem of noise, particularly in respect of data transmission by data terminals. The term is also used to describe duplicated data in files, which should be eliminated as far as possible, particularly in integrated files forming the structure of a database (*see* VII, **2**).

BUSINESS MODELS AND SIMULATION

24. Business models. When developing computerised systems a systems analyst may have to experiment with the existing system to understand its behaviour under varying conditions of operation. One approach to solving specific problems inherent in particular business systems is to construct a model of the system. Variables and constraints in business systems are represented in models, symbolically, in the form of algorithms or algebraic equations. By this means they may be subjected to statistical or mathematical analysis, in order to observe their behaviour when subjected to changing variables: this, then, enables optimum solutions to particular problems to be obtained. This is actually experimenting with models as an aid to studying real life situations and is less costly and speedier than experimenting with the real life system itself. Different combinations of variables may be fitted into the model and the results observed.

As an example, a model of a stock control system may be prepared for experimentation purposes, perhaps to optimise the investment in stocks. Variations in lead time and usage rates may be established from historical information and applied to the model, progressively changing the variables one at a time. It will then be possible to observe:

(a) The number of occasions when items would be out of stock.

(b) The number of occasions the maximum stock level may be exceeded.

(c) The average investment of working capital in stocks for varying stock levels.

(d) The effect on stock levels through changes in safety stock levels, re-order levels, order quantities, lead times and usage rates.

When a computer is used to process the data, several years' operations may be obtained within a matter of hours.

Problems associated with the construction of models for complex systems arise from the need to ensure that variables and constraints are representative of the real life situation. Only in this way will a model react in a similar way to the real situation.

Models are often over-simplified, because of the difficulties encountered in identifying all variables and their relationships. Models are dynamic, in the sense that they can be used repeatedly to predict the results of different situations when different values are assigned to variables. It is possible to construct models accurately but assign values to variables inaccurately, which prevents accurate results from being obtained in respect of a systems behaviour.

25. Simulation. When experimenting with a model, the behaviour of the real life system is being simulated. In some instances, however, a system cannot be specified in precise algorithms, because the system behaves in a non-predictable manner, i.e. it is a stochastic or probabilistic system. In such cases, historical data or estimated values have to be collected regarding the frequency with which events occur and Monte Carlo techniques used to simulate the random behaviour of the system. In this way, queueing problems may be resolved regarding the number of check-out points required in a supermarket, ship arrivals requiring berthing facilities and aircraft arrivals and departures requiring servicing facilities, etc. (*see* Appendix III).

PROGRESS TEST 11

1. Define the term "systems analysis". **(1)**

2. Since the analysis stage of a project is the foundation on which design can be built, it is a critical factor in eventual success. Discuss this point of view and propose methods of analysis aimed at achieving maximum effectiveness. **(1–11)**

(I.A.M. W1974, Part B, Q8)

3. Outline relationships and differences between systems analysis and O. & M. analysis. **(2)**

4. What knowledge, skills, and attributes are desirable in staff engaged in the development of administrative systems? **(3)**

(I.A.M. S1974, Part B, Q5)

5. "Depending upon the complexity and type of system to be investigated, some projects require a team of analysts." Discuss this statement. **(4)**

6. Indicate the differing approach which may be adopted by O. & M. and systems analysts in the development of systems. **(5)**

7. Specify important objectives of systems design. **(6)**

8. Outline essential factors which should be considered for the effective design of computer systems. **(7)**

9. What factors should be taken into account when designing computer runs? **(8)**

10. Indicate various approaches which may be used for the effective design of computer systems. **(9–11)**

11. Some writers advocate a "top-down" approach to systems development, whilst others recommend a "bottom-up" approach. Contrast and explain the bases for these opposing views. **(11)**

(I.A.M. W1974, Part B, Q5)

12. Discuss the need for documentation covering the analysis and design of systems. **(12–17)**

13. Indicate the structure of a typical systems specification. **(13)**

14. Define and indicate the purpose of the following techniques used in systems analysis and design:

(*a*) System flow chart

(b) Computer run chart

(c) Decision tables. **(14–17)**

15. Define the term "cybernetics", stating why a systems analyst needs to be familiar with cybernetic concepts. **(18, 19)**

16. In cybernetics, one of the central ideas is that of "feedback". What do you understand by the term and what relevance does it have to commercial systems? **(20)**

(I.A.M. S1975, Paper B, Q8)

17. Define the following cybernetic terms:

(a) Feedback

(b) Homeostasis

(c) Noise

(d) Redundancy. **(20–23)**

18. The elimination of duplicate work or information is normally regarded as one of the main aims of a systems analyst. Discuss circumstances where duplication may be justified and outline the principles that the analyst should follow in such situations. **(22, 23)**   **(I.A.M. S1975, Paper A, Q5)**

19. Indicate the relevance of business models and simulation to the work of a systems analyst. **(24, 25)**

CHAPTER XII

Monitoring Business Systems: Internal Auditing

THE FUNCTION OF INTERNAL AUDITING

1. Internal auditing defined. Internal auditing is a monitoring activity with responsibility to management for assessing the effectiveness of accounting and other business systems. It is a means of obtaining an independent assessment of business operations as a whole and is not limited to the operations of any particular function.

2. Authority of internal auditors. The audit function has no executive authority, it is purely an advisory activity. The function does not have responsibility for the development of new control systems, as this is the responsibility of systems development staff. Internal auditors should be consulted, however, about proposed changes, and their advice should actually be sought regarding the control element in any proposed changes, as they are independent assessors of the adequacy of control procedures.

In this respect, they make a valuable contribution by indicating the essential control elements which should be incorporated in any system or procedure. Internal auditors have authority to inspect all business documents and records, and authority to ensure that all business assets are adequately safeguarded by insurance policies for insurable risks, and that effective measures are taken to avoid fraud.

AUDIT PLANNING AND REPORTING

3. Audit planning. The auditing activity utilises valuable man-power resources and accordingly it should be used in the most effective way. To this end, each audit should be planned and the following considerations taken into account.

(*a*) A time schedule should be prepared for all auditing

activities, indicating the time individual audits should take and the timing of their occurrence.

(b) Assessment of problem areas, types of problem, and their relative importance with regard to the effective operation of the business.

(c) Allocation of appropriate audit staff to defined auditing activities, in view of the experience required for their effective review.

(d) Defining the appropriate audit trail for specific types of audit.

(e) Indication of the testing and sampling techniques to be applied during the course of an audit and evaluating the results obtained.

4. Audit reporting. The conclusions derived from conducting an audit in any sphere of the business should be included in a report to management, thus bringing to its attention any matter of which it should be aware and any action to be taken.

The report should state the actual or potential problems encountered, or likely to be encountered, together with constructive criticism and suggestions to resolve the problems actually in existence, or which are likely to materialise, if some action is not taken.

TYPES OF AUDIT ACTIVITY

5. Accounts and records audit. This type of audit is intended to discover errors and attempts at fraudulent conversion as soon as possible, and to minimise the amount of detail to be checked by external auditors during the course of the annual audit.

The auditing of accounting records also facilitates the preparation of accurate management control reports during the financial year, as periodic audits will, no doubt, discover errors and other inaccuracies, whilst the overall situation is current and not historical.

This audit will facilitate the following requirements:

(a) Ensuring that established accounting principles are being applied to the processing of accounting records.

(b) Testing the effectiveness of internal check procedures.

(c) Testing the accuracy of entries on source documents which is an essential pre-requisite for accurate accounting records.

(*d*) Ensuring that account codes are accurately recorded on all relevant records and documents.

(*e*) Ensuring that transaction data are recorded in correct accounts, i.e. no errors of commission.

(*f*) Ensuring that transaction data are recorded in correct types of account: that there are no errors of principle, i.e. revenue expenditure is not posted to Capital account.

(*g*) Assessing the suitability of control ratios generated from the accounting records.

6. Personnel audit. Auditing in this respect is mainly concerned with reviewing procedures relating to personnel matters, such as assessing the suitability and effectiveness of the following factors:

(*a*) The methods and techniques employed for personnel selection.

(*b*) The methods of job evaluation employed.

(*c*) The measures taken to minimise labour turnover.

(*d*) The criteria for selecting personnel for promotion.

(*e*) Assessing the suitability of personnel for defined tasks.

7. Methods and procedure audit. The primary aim of this type of audit is to assess the suitability of the methods and procedures employed for specific activities and reporting apparently unacceptable situations to the Organisation and Methods section, for initiating a detailed investigation. The O. & M. section is an advisory body similar to that of internal auditing, and it is interesting to note that advisors in this case advise the advisors! The basic elements of this type of audit are as follows:

(*a*) Follow-up after the installation of a new method or procedure, to ensure that it is operating smoothly and in the prescribed manner outlined in the procedure manual supplied by the O. & M. section (*see* X, **26, 27**).

(*b*) Assessing the adequacy of the filing equipment and methods in use.

(*c*) Assessing the suitability of personnel for the tasks assigned to them.

(*d*) Reviewing the organisation structure and its suitability for the activities performed.

(*e*) Reviewing the suitability of the forms used.

In addition to the audit activities outlined above, other audits which may be carried out include cost audit, management audit, forms audit, stores audit, stock-taking audit, fixed assets audit and cash audit, etc.

AUDITING COMPUTERISED PROCEDURES

8. Black box technique. In the early days of auditing computerised procedures, auditors adopted what is known as the black box approach because the technique does not necessitate a knowledge of computers or programming. The computer was referred to as the black box and the technique adopted was to audit round, not through, the computer, which was treated as a mysterious box of tricks of no concern to the auditing activity.

This approach was necessary, due to lack of knowledge of computers by auditors generally. Auditing round the computer is generally satisfactory for batch processing applications, as hard copy (printed output) is obtained automatically at various stages of processing. The printed output consists of control lists, transactions applied lists and lists of balances on accounts, etc. in addition to basic documents and management reports. Lists of balances replace the normal accounting ledgers.

To audit the results of computer operations, the output from the computer is compared with pre-calculated results of a sample of records, and if there is no discrepancy it is assumed that the output produced is satisfactory.

With the development of real-time systems, however, hard copy output is more the exception than the rule, as data is directly input by keyboard terminals (*see* IX, **15–18**). The data is then processed and the results displayed on the screen of a VDU if necessary. It is possible to obtain a hard copy of the information displayed if it is necessary to retain it for any purpose. Very often, in such instances, input data are only required for updating the relevant master files stored either on magnetic discs or magnetic cards, etc. and information is retrieved on request by means of remote enquiry facilities.

The disappearance of the traditional audit trail, in such instances, is the fundamental problem for auditors concerned with auditing computer-based systems, as source documents are also often eliminated and the records stored on magnetic media are invisible to the naked eye. Such records replace the normal accounting records and they may only be accessed in the manner indicated above.

It is possible for an auditor to have the contents of master files printed out, particularly those relating to real-time applications, but this would create a large volume of printed output which would occupy the computer for a considerable time, largely for an unproductive purpose. It is also doubtful if the auditor would have sufficient time at his disposal to check the output to any great extent (*see* **10**).

9. Test packs. Test data containing valid and invalid data may be punched into cards and processed under the control of the auditor to enable him to detect any shortcomings in the computer program.

Data contained in a test pack is pre-calculated, to enable the results to be compared with the results produced by the computer. By this means, the effectiveness of the program can be evaluated, as the program should be capable of dealing with abnormal data as well as routine recurring data. The application of test packs requires considerable knowledge of computerised systems (*see* VIII, **14**).

10. Audit packages. An audit package is basically a program specially prepared and fully tested for auditing computer systems. One particular package obtained from ICL is called Auditfind, and it enables selected records to be extracted from a master file, e.g. those relating to wages which have exceeded a specified amount in a specified pay period. The records may then be printed out and examined by the auditor. The auditor must be fully conversant with the package and computer operations in order to apply the technique effectively.

11. Checks and controls. It is essential to incorporate checks and controls in computer programs to provide self-checking facilities for the purpose of signalling invalid data, so that it may be checked, corrected and re-presented for processing. It is pointless processing faulty data, as the results cannot be any more accurate than the initial data.*

Auditors need to observe internal check principles with computerised systems, as it is still necessary to avoid collusion to perpetuate fraud. Accordingly, it is necessary to separate the activities of data origination, data control, data preparation, data processing, systems analysis and design, as well as programming (*see* IV, **2**(*e*)).

Auditors should also ensure that procedures are suitably documented, and that amendments are formally recorded and

* Garbage in, garbage out (GIGO).

routed through the internal audit department. Systems documentation, in general, consists of the following:

(a) Procedure narrative of current and proposed system.
(b) Procedure charts.
(c) System flowcharts.
(d) Run diagrams.
(e) Program flowcharts and coding sheets.
(f) Program print-out.
(g) Operating instructions.
(h) Testing routines.
(i) Error routines.
(j) Program modifications.
(k) Computer log.
(See XI, 12, 13.)

12. Auditing review of computer applications. The factors which should be reviewed in computerised applications are many and varied, but the following outline will serve to indicate the essential factors which should be subjected to scrutiny.

(a) *Data control.*

(i) Ensuring that documents are received in identifiable batches, complete with control totals and identification of the initiating departments.

(ii) Ensuring that source documents are complete in respect of relevant data fields, particularly with regard to the "key" identifying field, and that all data is legible.

(iii) Ensuring that all batches received for processing are recorded in a control register.

(iv) Ensuring that invalid data is detected by a validation program.

(v) Ensuring that output reports and schedules from the computer room are recorded in a control register and despatched promptly to the user department(s).

(vi) Ensuring that computer-generated control totals are compared with batch control totals and suitable action taken when they do not agree (*see* IX, 13, 14).

(b) *Computer management.*

(i) Assessing whether job schedules are prepared to ensure that jobs are completed at scheduled times.

(ii) Ensuring that company policy is adhered to.

(iii) Assessing the degree of involvement of the data processing manager in the activities of a steering committee.

(*c*) *Storage of master file records.*

(*i*) Assessing the adequacy of data storage facilities with regard to volumes of records stored, accessibility and effectiveness of processing with regard to the "hit" rate (*see* IX, 5).

(*ii*) Assessing the degree of protection provided by the technique of file generation or copying for reconstructing files when records are destroyed or corrupted (*see* IX, 6).

(*iii*) Assessing the adequacy of storage facilities for the safe custody of files (*see* Appendix IV).

(*d*) *Audit trail.* Tracing a sample of processing from source documents, through master files to output reports and/or documents.

(*e*) *Operations.*

(*i*) Establishing whether computer operating instructions are updated formally to conform with the changes required for specific applications.

(*ii*) Assessing the effectiveness of file maintenance procedures and computer program validation routines (*see* IX, 8).

(*iii*) Assessing the efficiency of procedures for dealing with program modification requests and whether they are formally presented in writing.

PROGRESS TEST 12

1. Define the function of internal auditing. **(1)**
2. Define the authority of internal auditors. **(2)**
3. Why is it necessary to plan internal audits? **(3)**
4. What is the purpose of audit reporting? **(4)**
5. State the nature of an accounts and records audit. **(5)**
6. State the nature of a personnel audit. **(6)**
7. What do you understand by the term "systems audit"? Describe the objectives and essential components of such an audit. **(7)** (I.A.M. S1974, Part B, Q6)
8. Many people believe that the lack of conventional records and files when using a computer for processing clerical systems makes the control and audit of those systems unsatisfactory. Discuss this belief and describe the techniques available for effective control and audit. **(8–12)**
(I.A.M. S1973, Paper 1, Q7)
9. It is contended by some authorities that fraud is more easily carried out and detection made more difficult in a computer-based

system. Discuss this view and describe procedures that may be established to minimise the risk.   **(10, 11)**

(I.A.M. W1973, Paper 1, Q2)

10. Suggest and justify general principles that a designer should follow in minimising the possibility of fraud in a system of which you have some knowledge.   **(11)**   (I.A.M. S1975, Paper B, Q6)

Examination Technique

Examination questions in respect of business systems are generally of a practical nature, requiring a knowledge of well-defined principles and relative advantages and disadvantages of alternative methods. Those, for instance, in respect of accounting systems relating to the use of manual, mechanical and electronic methods of data processing, including the possible use of a computer bureau instead of an in-house computer. Other types of question may be conceptual in nature, requiring a knowledge of cybernetic principles, systems integration and databases.

The subject of business systems is very wide and students should always take care to demonstrate the practical and wider implications of what may appear to be very narrow questions. It is good practice to answer questions from experience, whenever possible, supported by accepted principles within the context of specific questions.

The examination candidate is recommended to observe the following points:

(*a*) Read each question thoroughly before attempting an answer, in order to avoid any initial misunderstanding of the requirements of the question. A good answer to the wrong question does not score marks.

(*b*) Allocate sufficient time to answering each question. It can be detrimental to examination success to omit an answer to a required question completely, through spending too much time on other questions. It is much better to have a fairly complete answer on all questions rather than no answer at all on some of them.

(*c*) Having determined the requirements of each question, the first one to be attempted should be selected. It is good practice before committing yourself to the answer paper to jot down main headings or topics to be covered on a scrap pad. By this means, initial thoughts may be clarified and the full scope of the question appreciated.

(*d*) The answer may then be written on the answer paper, observing the following points:

(*i*) Write legibly to enable the examiner to interpret your answer easily.

(*ii*) Show a good command of English, sentence structure and grammar.

(*iii*) Outline the answer on the basis of topic or subject headings sub-analysed as appropriate as follows:

  (*a*)
    (*i*)
    (*ii*)
  (*b*)
  (*c*)
    (*i*)
    (*ii*)
    (*iii*)

By this means the examiner can easily assess the points being made and can more readily appreciate their relevance and award marks accordingly.

(*iv*) Keep to the subject and be as concise as possible, without unnecessary padding—you either know the subject or you do not. Make sure you do, before sitting the examination, even if only to save examination fees.

(*e*) Allow sufficient time to read the answers before handing in the paper, so that corrections can be effected.

(*f*) Some answers require the presentation of a flowchart or procedure chart and it is important to use drawing aids in their construction, i.e. charting symbol templates or coins (for circles), and a rule (for straight lines). Neatness of presentation is very important if maximum marks are to be gained.

Flow Chart Symbols

Below are indicated the five basic ASME symbols devised by the American Society of Mechanical Engineers. The symbols provide a form of shorthand for describing the nature of each activity in a procedure. Other charting symbols may be used when appropriate to describe other features of a procedure. Such symbols are also illustrated.

The five basic flowcharting symbols:

Inspection. The chief result of inspection is verification of quantity and/or quality.
— checking letters for errors and appearance
— checking the accuracy of a calculation
— ensuring that relevant details are included on a form and are correct
— comparing documents for accuracy of data
— checking quantity produced of a particular document.

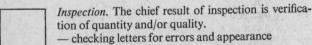

Transportation. The chief result of transportation is movement.
— delivering a letter by messenger
— transporting invoices on a conveyer
— transferring a document from one department to another
— movement of personnel between work stations.
The distance moved may be shown on the left of the symbol. The direction of movement is indicated by the direction of the arrow.

Storage (Filing). The chief result of storage is deliberate retention.
— filing documents on completion of action
— replacing ledger cards in a container after a posting run.

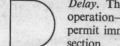

Delay. The chief result of delay is deferring an operation—when, for instance, conditions do not permit immediate attention to work flowing into a section.

— a letter awaiting attention

— a letter on a desk awaiting signature

— authorising payment of purchase invoices delayed because of non-compatibility of goods received with those invoiced.

Operation. Chief result of an operation is to accomplish or further a procedure.

— reading a letter for information

— calculating a price extension

— filling in a form

— signing a document.

If desired, the nature of the operation may be indicated by inserting a letter in the circle e.g.

 — clerical operation

 — machine operation

 — typewriter operation.

Other charting symbols:

TITLE
REF

Title box. Describes and indicates the entry point of a document or person in a procedure.

TITLE 1	TITLE 2	TITLE 3	TITLE 4
REF 1	REF 2	REF 3	REF 4

Multiple title box. Describes and indicates the entry

point of a multiple set of documents, e.g. documents
assembled in a set (such as an invoice document set)
ready for use.

Lines. Show routes of travel and interrelationships
between documents, persons or actions thus:

— *vertical solid line.* Links the operations performed
on a document or by a person in sequence.

— *multiple solid lines.* Where two or three documents
travel together and action is taken on them simultaneously, vertical lines should be drawn for each
document.

— *horizontal solid line.* Indicates bringing together,
or separation, of documents or persons.

— *vertical barred line.* Where more than three
documents are involved it is convenient to use this
symbol to indicate links between operations.

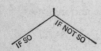

— *branching line.* For alternative routes,
because of varying circumstances.

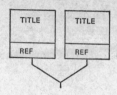 *Alternative title boxes.* The choice of one or two documents according to varying circumstances.

 Horizontal dotted line. Where one document has an effect on another the associated activities are joined by a dotted line.

 Vertical dotted line. Shows where a document is temporarily out of action.

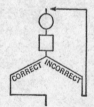 *Branching dotted lines.* Alternatives to indicate variations in effect on different documents.

Over-pass line. Shows an over-pass when lines cross.

Correction. Correction of errors is indicated by a branch to the right of the chart, the branch being carried back so that all activities required for the correction are contained in the loop.

 Limits of investigation. Sometimes a document may continue beyond the boundaries of the investigation.

 Repeats. Repeating activities are indicated by a branch to the left of the chart, the branch being carried back so that all activities required for the repeat are contained in the loop.

Before attempting to chart details it is important to decide whether the activities to be recorded relate to a person, a document or a group of related documents.

General flowchart symbols for the construction of computer run charts:

Punched cards—input or output.

Punched paper tape—input or output.

Operation—processing step.

Report—printed output.

Magnetic tape—input or output.

Magnetic drum on-line storage—input or output.

Magnetic disc on-line storage—input or output.

Flow lines.

NCC flowchart symbols for the construction of computer run charts:

Operation—processing step.

Computer backing storage—input or output.

Data transfers—input or output. Generalised symbol.

General program (computer procedure) flowchart symbols for the construction of computer procedure flowcharts:

Terminal—start, halt, delay, stop, or interrupt.

Connector—to connect together different sections of a flowchart.

Decision—to denote alternative actions.

Operations—processing step.

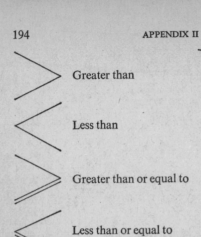

Greater than

Less than

Greater than or equal to

Less than or equal to

used in combination
with decision symbol.

Flow lines

APPENDIX III

Case Study 1—Real Time Control of Steel Making

The system outlined below is based on the systems specification for the Blooming Mill System of the Patent Shaft Steelworks Ltd., and is reproduced by their kind permission.

The objective of the system is to eliminate pieces in the Blooming Mill either partially or completely, i.e. to reduce that portion of the ingot unallocated to customers' orders. The disadvantage of pieces is twofold:

(a) *Loss in Plate Mill yield.* Since a piece is not tailor-made to an order it produces scrap in the Plate Mill, in addition to the unavoidable side and end scrap.

(b) *Loss in Plate Mill throughput.* A lower tonnage of pieces than slabs can be rolled, in any time period, for a given order mix. An order consisting of slabs, all of the same dimensions, can be rolled faster in the Plate Mill than a like order of pieces. With slabs, a rolling pattern can be developed so that rolling time is decreased for the second and subsequent slabs in a batch. With a batch of pieces, all different sizes, no pattern is possible.

1. The manual system. The weight of ingots varies and when an ingot is cogged in the Blooming Mill, its actual length is unknown until it reaches the shear and has been topped and tailed. With the manual system, the allocation of ingots is pre-planned, assuming a theoretical running length, and the last portion of an ingot is not allocated to any order. The length of this piece is unknown until shearing is completed and at a later stage must be matched as close as possible to an order item.

2. The real-time system. With the real-time system it is proposed to provide a terminal at the shear, so that the planning decision as to how the ingot is cut up is left until the length has been measured and input to the computer. The computer will then search the order book for orders that match the chemical analysis of the ingot and calculate that combination of order slab lengths

195

which produces minimum scrap, thereby eliminating the need for a piece, providing the amount of scrap is not excessive. This method will result in a loss in Blooming Mill yield, but this is far outweighed financially by the gains in Plate Mill yield and throughput that will result.

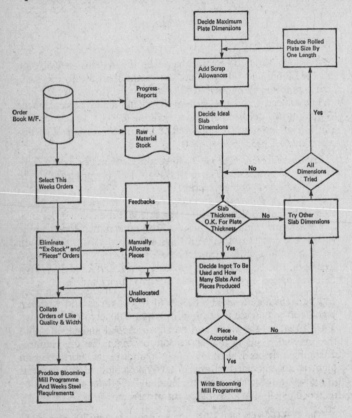

In order to introduce this method of planning, information other than ingot length must be collected. To match ingots to orders, it is necessary to know the analysis. Data must also be collected about heats (quantities of metal in the Furnace for melting and refining), made in the Steel Plant and heats arriving and being charged in the Blooming Mill. The cogger must be provided with cogging sections, the shearman with shearing lengths, and so on. The full list of terminals required is as follows:

(a) A teletype in the Steel Plant office to output steel orders from the Planning department and input details of heats made.

(b) A VDU in the laboratory to input analysis details.

(c) A display terminal in the Soaking Pit recorders office to collect details of heat arrivals and charging.

(d) Eight terminals, one for each pit, along the soaking pit landing, to input which position within the pit is being discharged.

(e) A display terminal in the coggers cabin, to display the cogging section required and for the cogger to indicate when cogging is completed.

(f) Two terminals, one either side of shear, for input of the ingot running length.

(g) Display terminals for the shearsman and shear operator to output shearing and for the shear operator to indicate details when each slab is sheared.

(h) Display terminal for the marker.

(i) Display terminal for piler operator.

(j) Teletype for slab yard stocktaker to output and input stacking information.

(k) Teletype for the foreman to print information about occurrences that require attention, e.g. a heat being charged before the analysis has arrived.

(l) Two printers in the foreman's office, to output security details about cogging and shearing for all ingots charged into the pits, to be used in case of computer failure.

(m) In addition, a VDU and teletype will be provided for the Production controller. The controller will play an extremely important part in the system, being able to deal with all extraordinary situations, e.g. making the decision about a heat arriving in the Blooming Mill for which there are no, or insufficient, orders. He will order steel, control the size of the order-book on the mini-computer and be able to amend any of the system files. He will provide the system with the flexibility required.

3. Design concepts. The decision to change from a pre-allocation to a re-allocation method for shearing slabs implied the use of an on-line computer system. The financial advantages of the re-allocation techniques were deduced from results provided by a simulation model of the proposed re-allocation procedure (*see* Blooming Mill allocation model on p. 196).

Elementary considerations of the amount of calculation required by the re-allocation method and the time available for carrying these out, showed that automatic computation is required and on-line (as opposed to batch) processing was also necessary.

The next point to be decided was the extent of the system. It was decided to include all those activities, from ordering steel to slab piling operations in the stockyard. A number of computer terminals have been assigned to locations in the Blooming Mill, Steel Plant and Planning office in order to collect and display data concerning the state of operations in those areas.

These considerations established the need for a computer system, capable of handling input and output for a number of terminals simultaneously and allowing a number of separate tasks to be active at the same time.

The very important consideration of system reliability has been satisfied by:

(*a*) Duplicating the central processor and communication paths.

(*b*) Allowing the functions of one terminal to be taken over by another.

(*c*) Advance scheduling (pre-allocation) to provide back-up solutions for ingot shearing for some time ahead.

The above considerations led to the choice of the twin PDP-11/40 processor system, including terminals, disc and magnetic tape running under the control of the RSX-11D operating system.

The important features of the total design can be deduced by considering answers to the following questions:

(*a*) Which activities and decisions are to be carried out by people and which by machine?

(*b*) Can the total system be split up into natural sub-sections and if so how is this to be achieved?

Considering the first question, a basic principle has been to design the system so that people and computers each perform those activities to which they are best suited. Thus, the computer system deals with the vast majority of routine situations, carries out data collection and updating of files and performs the necessary calculations in the re-allocation phase.

This leaves the people controlling the system to handle the

exception conditions and, in general, to make use of their knowledge and experience to handle such situations. Important consequences of this approach are:

(a) People will not feel that they have become unimportant. This will be of great value in ensuring that the system is accepted, since people will be disposed to use it rather than react against it.

(b) It saves a great deal of time which would have had to be spent in producing programs to cover those few, exceptional conditions which rarely arise. To have adopted the "complete automation" approach would not only have taken disproportionately longer (due to the effect mentioned above), but would also have made the system rigid and less acceptable to the people involved.

(c) The total system possesses that important quality "flexibility", that is, the ability to maintain performance under many different operational conditions, such as partial equipment failure, unusual mill conditions caused by plant failure, etc. This is a direct consequence of having designed the system to be a "helpful assistant" rather than a "dictatorial master".

4. Simulation. Incorporated in the real-time system will be a number of parameters that can be varied to produce different results from the system. Among these parameters are:

(a) Maximum length of ingot over which optimisation takes place.

(b) Maximum number of orders that may be considered for reallocation to any one ingot.

(c) Limits on scrap produced.

(d) The number of sizes into which an order may be cogged and the limits on those sizes.

In order to determine the effects of these parameters on any situation, it is proposed to modify the Blooming Mill allocation model, to work with the live order and cast files from the real-time system. This will enable production management to amend any parameters and compare what would have happened over a shift or week, given the new parameters, with what actually happened given the existing parameters.

5. System interface. The Blooming Mill has several external interfaces:

(a) *Steel Plant.* Steel requirements are output from the system to the Steel Plant, and details of heats made are input.

(*b*) *Laboratory*. Analysis details for all heats made in the Steel
Plant are input to the system from the Laboratory. The Laboratory is also able to check the analysis for any cast held within the
system.

(*c*) *1900 Program Suites*. Orders input via the 1900 Order Entry
suite and processed by the Mill Planning suite are passed across
to the system at the request of the Production controller.

(*d*) *Plate Mill Planning*. At the end of each shift, details of all
slabs put down in the slabyard will be printed. This information
will be passed across to the Plate Mill Planner.

(*e*) *Management Reports*. At the end of each shift or week, a
number of reports will be printed for the management. These
include many of the reports currently produced by hand, e.g.
shift reports, soaking pits weekly analysis, B2 books etc. In
addition, reports will be produced on performance of the system,
discrepancies between steel produced and arriving in the Blooming Mill, etc.

6. Hardware. The computer system consists of two parts:

(*a*) A duplexed PDP 11-40 computer configuration with local
peripheral equipment (*see* Fig. showing Control Computer
Equipment on p. 201).

(*b*) A remote terminal sub-system connected by a communication network to the computer system (*see* Fig. showing General
Cable Layout on p. 202).

Communications between terminals and computer will be by
specially laid cable which will provide alternative paths to
minimise the risk of mechanical damage to the cable causing a
failure of the system.

(*a*) *Central Computer Configuration*. Each processor has
"64 K" (65,556) words of core storage, each word being 16 bits.
Allows segmentation of core storage for multiple-user environ-
ments and provides effective hardware protection of memory
segments.

(*b*) *Inter-processor buffer*. This communication channel is
required for two purposes:

(*i*) To enable the watch-dog timers to interrogate the processors and determine if failure has occurred.

(*ii*) To enable file updating data to be passed between the
processors.

(*c*) *The Unibus link* is a half duplex communication channel
which can connect together two PDP-II computers which are up

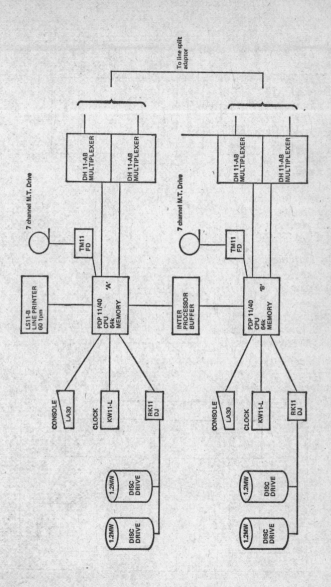

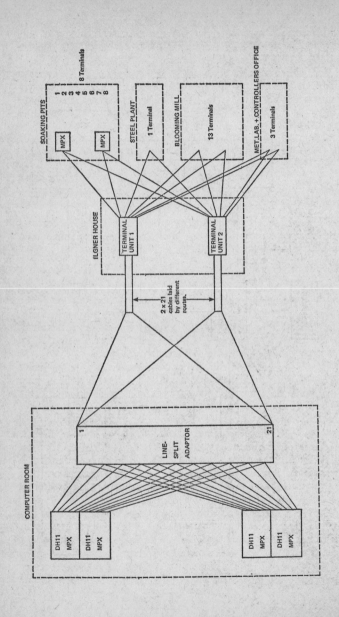

to 30 metres apart. Either single words of data, or blocks of data up to 32K words long, can be transmitted. The transfer rate can be up to 500,000 words per second.

(*d*) *Programmable Multiplexer*. Two of these units are attached to the unibus of each processor. Each unit enables 16 asynchronous communications lines to be connected to a single PDP-II. Each line can have its own transmission characteristics which can be changed by programmed instructions.

(*e*) *Disc drive and controller*. This is known as the DEC pack cartridge disc system. The unit consists of a disc drive controller, plus the first drive. Up to seven additional disc drives can be added to the controller. The disc system consists of disc cartridges of 1.2 million 16 bit word capacity mounted on each drive. A moving head mechanism is used to access data.

The central computer configuration consists of other features and devices in addition to those indicated which have been described as a matter of interest.

7. Special Considerations.

(*a*) *Order Priority Structure*. When an order enters the system, it will carry a priority of ø, 1 or 2 which will be allocated by the Sales Department. For each day that the order remains incomplete in the system, its priority will be increased up to a maximum of 5. Priorities of 6 and 7 will also exist to be allocated at the discretion of the Production controller.

Priority 6 will result in that order being chosen as the target order for the first ingot with matching steel entering the system, provided the ingot size was correct (i.e. that only one piece would result from a slab and piece solution). Priority 7 will have the same result as priority 6, except that it will be chosen as a prime order regardless of considerations of yield and throughput.

Within a set of orders with the same numerical priority importance, a further priority ranking can be decided. Orders which have been started will have a greater priority than those that have not, and the nearer an order is to completion the greater its priority. In addition, orders for OMS have a lower priority than all other specifications. Orders are allocated to ingots within this priority sequence.

(*b*) *Dual Processor Operation*. Although a high degree of reliability can be expected from a single processor system, it would be possible for a failure to a component in that processor to result in a complete loss of the computer system. To overcome

this, a dual processor system will operate, with one providing
back-up for the other. However, the back-up processor operation
will not mirror that of the main machine; the software problems
involved would outweigh the limited advantage to be gained.
Instead, while the main machine is operating, a copy of the up-
to-date order file, pit file, ingot file and slabyard file will be maintained on the second processor. In addition, a back-up system
will be maintained giving cogging details and a slab and piece
solution for all ingots drawn from the pits.

In the case of a breakdown of the main processor, the back-up
machine can begin processing immediately. However, those
ingots in process in the mill, at the time of changeover, will be
processed as given by the back-up system, i.e. slab and piece
solution. With up-to-date files, the second machine can operate
as normal from the next ingot drawn from the pits.

There is also a slight chance that the back-up processor will
break down before the main machine has been repaired. To cover
this possibility, it is proposed to reserve a portion of the order
book, not normally available for allocation, and use this to find
a slab and piece solution for all ingots as they are charged into
the pits.

These details will be output to a security printer, located in an
office near to the Blooming Mill foreman. In the event of a dual
processor failure, the foreman can produce work sheets as at
present. This will provide a minimum of three hours work for the
Blooming Mill.

During this three hours, the order file on the 1900 will be updated from the logging tape and Blooming Mill programs produced against the eventuality that neither machine is repaired
before the printed security details are exhausted. If the programs
have to be used, the manual planning system will have to continue
until the end of the week, because of the unknown state of the
order book. Recovery will take place over the weekend, when
there is time for all the files to be updated.

In case the 1900 breaks down at the same time, jobs will be
tape based so that they can be run on any 1900 elsewhere.

(c) *Blooming Mill Allocation Model.* The objective of the model
is to simulate a method of working in the Blooming Mill whereby
the decision as to which slabs are sheared from an ingot is left
until the ingot has been cogged, topped and tailed, and its length
measured. By this method it is hoped to reduce that portion of the
ingots unallocated to customers' orders, i.e. to eliminate some of

the pieces cogged at present. The model is also used to determine the effects of this method of working on the number of orders started and completed during a shift, and on the slab size cogged for each order.

The input to the model consists of a file of orders for cogging and several casts of ingots. The model considers each ingot in turn and determines the size to which it is cogged and its length after it has been cogged, topped and tailed. The model then determines the best way to shear this into slabs from the order file, to minimize the length to be scrapped or if this length is excessive to cut a piece. (*See* XI, **24, 25**).

Case Study 2—On-Line Building Society Operations

The details which follow are based on an article that appeared in *Accountancy Age* on 6th December 1974 and are reproduced by kind permission of Haymarket Publishing Ltd.

There are many problems associated with the administration of a large building society and the Nationwide Building Society attributes its efficiency to the effective use of computers. Nationwide has long been conscious of the need for efficiency coupled with service to members and in the late 1940s it adopted the policy of decentralising its mortgage and investment accounts to branch offices throughout the country. As a result, each branch was able to offer an instant members' enquiry service, as well as being aware of its financial position at any time.

As time passed, Nationwide, in common with many others, became concerned about escalating staff costs and the difficulty of recruiting and retaining suitable personnel. This led, in 1966, to the introduction of a computerised accounting system.

The society experienced a substantial increase in general efficiency, along with a significant control over escalating staff costs. The computer system was very successful from a financial point of view, but for these benefits a price had to be paid—the centralisation of its accounting functions in London.

As with most other computers available at the time, Nationwide's machine operated a batch processing system (*see* IX, **13**, **14**), and all transactions and enquiries had to be sent each day to London by post. This eliminated the instant, on-the-spot branch service to members, formerly available through the society's policy of decentralisation.

Nationwide had been experiencing a steady growth and it became apparent that current equipment would be incapable of dealing with projected workloads, even though the London installation had been increased to two large computers and associated peripherals.

This gave Nationwide the opportunity to review its data processing requirements and resulted in a decision to expend over £2 million on a new computer system, to give it the best of both worlds—the retention of a centralised accounting system with inherent staff and cost savings, along with a return to the instant branch service through terminals linked to a central computer.

The society searched for a computer system which would satisfy the following criteria.

(*a*) Improve service to customers, branches and management.
(*b*) Be amenable to change.
(*c*) Incorporate hardware capable of meeting 1980 workloads.

Seven manufacturers made proposals, from which was selected the Sperry Univac 1110 on-line system. A major factor in favour of the Univac machine was the scope it offered for expansion. It would be uneconomic to install the full computing capacity now that will be needed in the future. With the Univac 1110, Nationwide are starting with the configuration needed at present which will be enlarged as necessary. This will not involve reprogramming or disruption of existing work.

The system will enable Nationwide to provide continuous service during office hours to a widespread network of terminals and to process a heavy load of accounting work currently dealt with by its London computer centre.

The on-line system, apart from improving service to members, obviates the need for a large and expensive central data preparation department. Also, because files are to be amended daily, important financial information required by senior management will always be up to date.

Implementation of the project is to be carried out in three stages starting in 1975:

Stage 1. There will be a total data collection system using terminals to enter details on savings, investment and mortgages from branches to the central computer at Swindon.

Stage 2. Provides for on-line enquiry facilities.

Stage 3. The development of a management information service.

The system will be able to deal with some two million investment and mortgage accounts which, on an average day, may generate 50,000 transactions, rising at peak periods to 90,000 transactions. These transactions will be used to amend customer records, stored on magnetic discs forming a possible database of over 2,500 million characters. The database will provide a

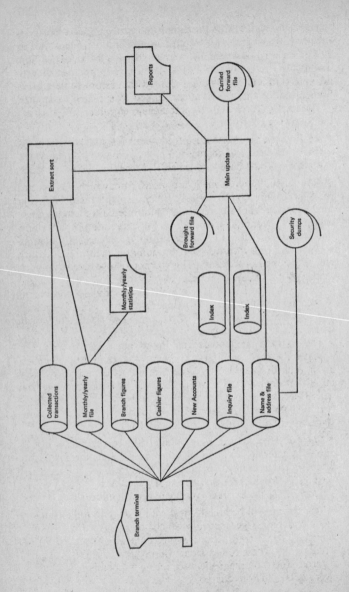

sophisticated management information system which will be developed through model building and simulation techniques to make the 1110 a true management tool (*see* VII and XI, **24, 25**).

One key decision which had to be made in the initial design stages of the system was how to distribute programmable processing capability, referred to as "intelligence", through the network. There were three main options:

(*a*) To retain all intelligence in the central computer.

(*b*) To delegate some intelligence to concentrators, placed at strategic locations in the network, to handle preprocessing of work from groups of terminals.

(*c*) To use intelligent terminals which can themselves carry out some elementary processing, such as the validation of data.

Nationwide chose the first of these three options for two main reasons:

(*a*) The computer configuration was powerful enough to handle the communications network, without slowing down the processing of primary tasks.

(*b*) The society's branches varied widely in both size and workload.

Ordinarily, such variation would require installation of several models of terminals. Instead, the society decided upon the use of Univac DCT 500 "idiot" terminals, whose cost is sufficiently low to justify installation in even the smallest branches. Those larger offices with a greater workload will be equipped with two or more terminals, as required. These terminals will be used purely as recorders, transmitters and receivers of data over Post Office telephone lines.

The machine itself operates as a multiprocessor, that is, it has two central processor units and two input/output units working as a single computer and sharing both main and extended memory and all peripheral devices. Should either processor develop a fault, the other takes over automatically, priority being given to on-line work from branches.

In addition there are three levels of security:

(*a*) Each cashier and terminal has its own security code without which the system cannot be used (*see* IX, **25**).

(*b*) At system level, extensive recovery routines have been built into programs to ensure that the system becomes operational again as soon as possible after a hardware or program failure.

(c) At whole-system level, all updating of files is carried out on magnetic tapes, which are then transferred overnight to random access magnetic discs. Security copies of the tapes are removed from the premises and stored off-site, as a safeguard against major disasters such as fires or, in this day and age, bombs.

By using magnetic tapes initially, rather than magnetic discs, a skeleton accounting service may be maintained on any alternative compatible computer system even though the installation may have been completely destroyed (*see* IX, **6** and the diagram of the computer system on p. 208).

Case Study 3—Catalogue Shopping in Retail Sales Operations

The details which follow are based on an article which appeared in *Accountancy Age* on 4th June 1976 and are reproduced by kind permission of Haymarket Publishing Ltd.

A new retailing operation has turned up in the High Street. Part supermarket—but without acres of self-service bins; part discount store—but providing a wide range of branded goods; part mail order—but without the Post Office connecting customer with retailer.

Already well-established in the US, this new approach to retailing is dominated in the UK by two chains.

(a) Argos Distributors (part of the Green Shield Group).
(b) Shoppers World (a division of F. W. Woolworths).

In the showroom, the goods featured in the catalogue—or at least, as many as can be fitted in—are displayed in cabinets, but are not available to be handled by the public. They are there to entice people into the showroom who have not seen the catalogue and, for those who have seen it, they reinforce the desire to purchase.

In the centre of the showroom is a table unit, with copies of the catalogue, pens and order forms. Customers fill in the order form with stock number, quantity and unit price from the catalogue, and take it to be processed by the sales assistants.

At this point two very different systems take over—a basically manual system at Shoppers World, and a mechanical one at Argos.

1. Shoppers World system. There are three parts to the Shoppers World order form, which is taken to the cash desk and given to the assistant. She checks that the price and product code agree with the catalogue and then disappears into the stockroom to find out if the goods are available.

If satisfied with his purchase, the customer pays and the order form is put into a cash register, which stamps the amount paid

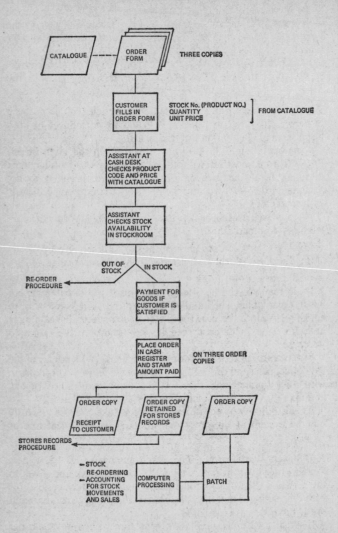

upon each of the three copies of the order form. One copy is given as a receipt to the customer. The second copy is kept for the store's records, and the bottom copy is batched and sent to the warehouse where it enters the computer and is used to re-order stock for the store.

It also initiates the accounting entries to record the stock movement and sale. So a manual system operates (see p. 212), the paperwork being completed by the customer, except at the warehouse.

Stock control at Shoppers World is in the hands of the sales assistants, who verify if the goods are available or not, whereas Argos have gone for a system of stock inquiry.

2. Argos system. In the large Argos branches, the Plessey lightpen system is used. This comprises four basic components:

(a) The master catalogue with the product numbers represented by machine readable "bar codes".

(b) The light-pen interrogation unit.

(c) The databank and console.

(d) The picking ticket printer.

When a customer presents his order at the cash desk, the assistant consults the master catalogue and finds the "bar code" corresponding to the product sought. The "bar code" is a series of lines of black type of various thicknesses which, when read, represent a number.

The reading is done by fibre optics contained in a pen-like handle, hence the term "light-pen". Taking the light-pen interrogation unit, she passes the light-pen over the "bar code" which enters the product code into the Plessey databank.

The databank contains all the product codes which are not in stock and, after comparing the number entered against the numbers of out of stock items, it flashes back to the interrogation unit either a "not in stock" indicator, or it gives a buzz to tell the assistant it is available. If available, it also prints out a picking ticket in the stock room, on the paper printer which shows the product number.

Also in the stock room with the databank and the ticket printer is the console. This unit is used to control the input and output from the databank. When an assistant finds that an item goes out of stock, she uses the console to enter the stock number into the databank memory, so that any further demands for that product will elicit the "out-of-stock" response.

Conversely, when stock is received which was out of stock at the store, the console is used to remove their numbers from the databank. A listing of all out-of-stock products in the databank can also be initiated from the console.

While the stock is being taken from the shelves, the customer is meeting the second bit of mechanisation. The cash registers which combine an ordinary cash register, a verifier and optical-character-encoder. The assistant enters the product number, which is verified to check that it is valid (using a check digit in the number), and the price. These are printed on the two-part order form completed by the customer, one copy for him, one copy for the shop.

The information is also recorded in a special optical font on paper tape in the cash register, for processing on the Green Shield computer at Head Office. Unlike the "bar codes" used in the master catalogue, the optical font is readable both by machine and man. Not only are sales recorded, though, but also all the unsatisfied inquiries for which the product was out of stock.

So total demand can be determined for each product and not just demand satisfied. This provides more information for stock re-ordering, which is controlled by each store's manager, rather than automatically re-ordered by computer.

In the smaller Argos stores, the investment in Plessey light-pen equipment is not justified and a "stockboard" system of stock control is employed. Here each stock item has its own pigeonhole on the board, in which cards are left showing either the goods are available, and if so how many, or that they are out-of-stock, in which case the card can show which item is the best substitute to offer the customer ("switch selling").

The system provides the following benefits:

(a) Faster customer turnaround in the stores at peak hours.

(b) Very tight control over stock and cash through the use of the special cash registers.

(c) At no time is the customer left alone while the goods are being searched for.

(d) Product demand can be more easily assessed.

The two Figs. outline the features of both systems and they are the author's interpretation, from the details provided in the article.

This type of retailing has the added advantage that shoplifting is not possible, which, of course, reduces the losses that are incurred by other types of retailing due to this problem.

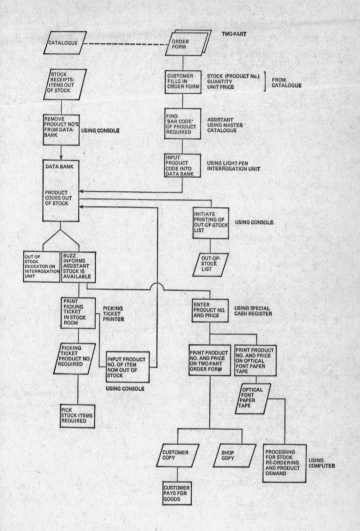

Index